ATI

by Torin Monaco

and

BOB

by Malachi Keel

Ati and Bob, two seminal characters of contemporary literature. Both defy the suffocating constraints of social convention to forge their own path. Both quest for self-definition, in defiance of the meager roles society has conscripted them. Ati, a bomb, is on a desperate search for his family, for solace. Turning to his friends in his hour of need, he is brutally pummelled with their pea shooters. It is always darkest before the dawn however, as Ati is suddenly reunited with his bomb family and promptly falls asleep.

And what can we say about Bob? His complexity, the emotional intricacy of his motivations is akin to Faulkner's characterization at the height of his powers. But we begin not in Faulkner's mystic south, but in contemporary America, somewhere in the Pacific Northwest, where a well-intentioned young man finds himself sent to the principle's office. What was his infraction? In a kafkaesque turn we never find out, for before any explanation emerges, a unicorn intervenes, whisking the intrepid Bob away from the school, over the rooftops, to finally arrive in a crystalline underground kingdom ruled by a terrifying monarch. Bob is immediately imprisoned and encounters the king as he is trying to sneak away to ride his unicorn to freedom. The final page gives a coda which reflects the genesis of the narrative: Bob's confrontation with the king and their mutual cries of alarm (AAAAAAAAAA) mirror the inciting incident, in which Bob and the principle utter the same mournful ululation. Ultimately, we see this cry as transcending its narrative function, The cry of "AAAAAAAAAAAA" is an atavistic assertion existence, an ontological statement on the meaning of human life. Aren't we all just calling "AAAAAAAAA" into the void?

-editor

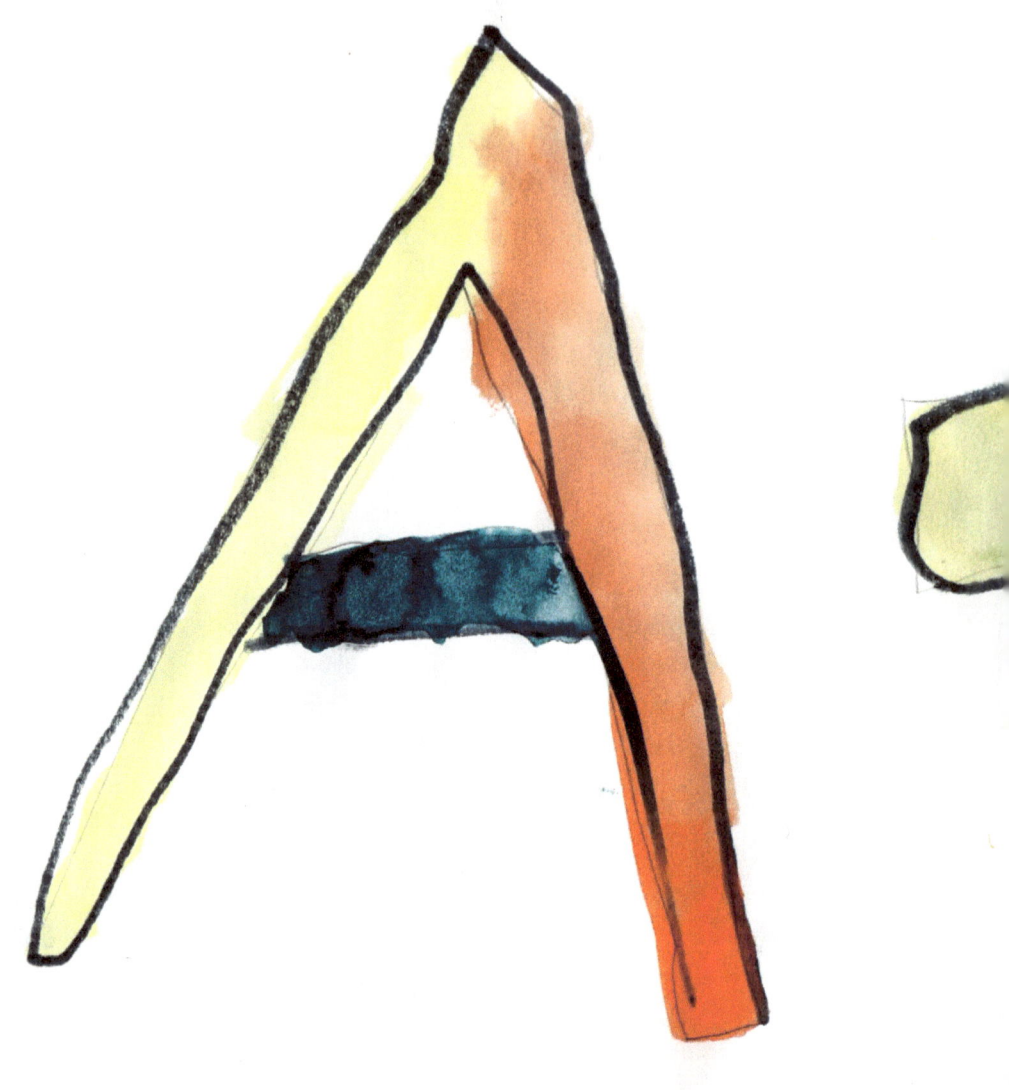

By torin
illustrate

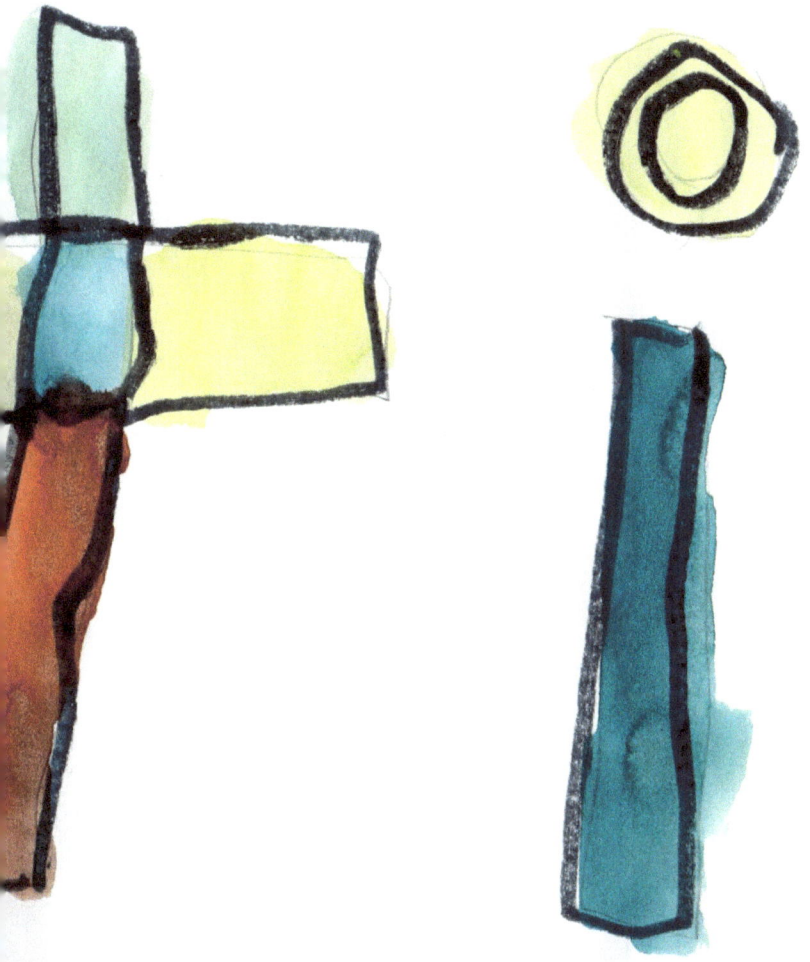

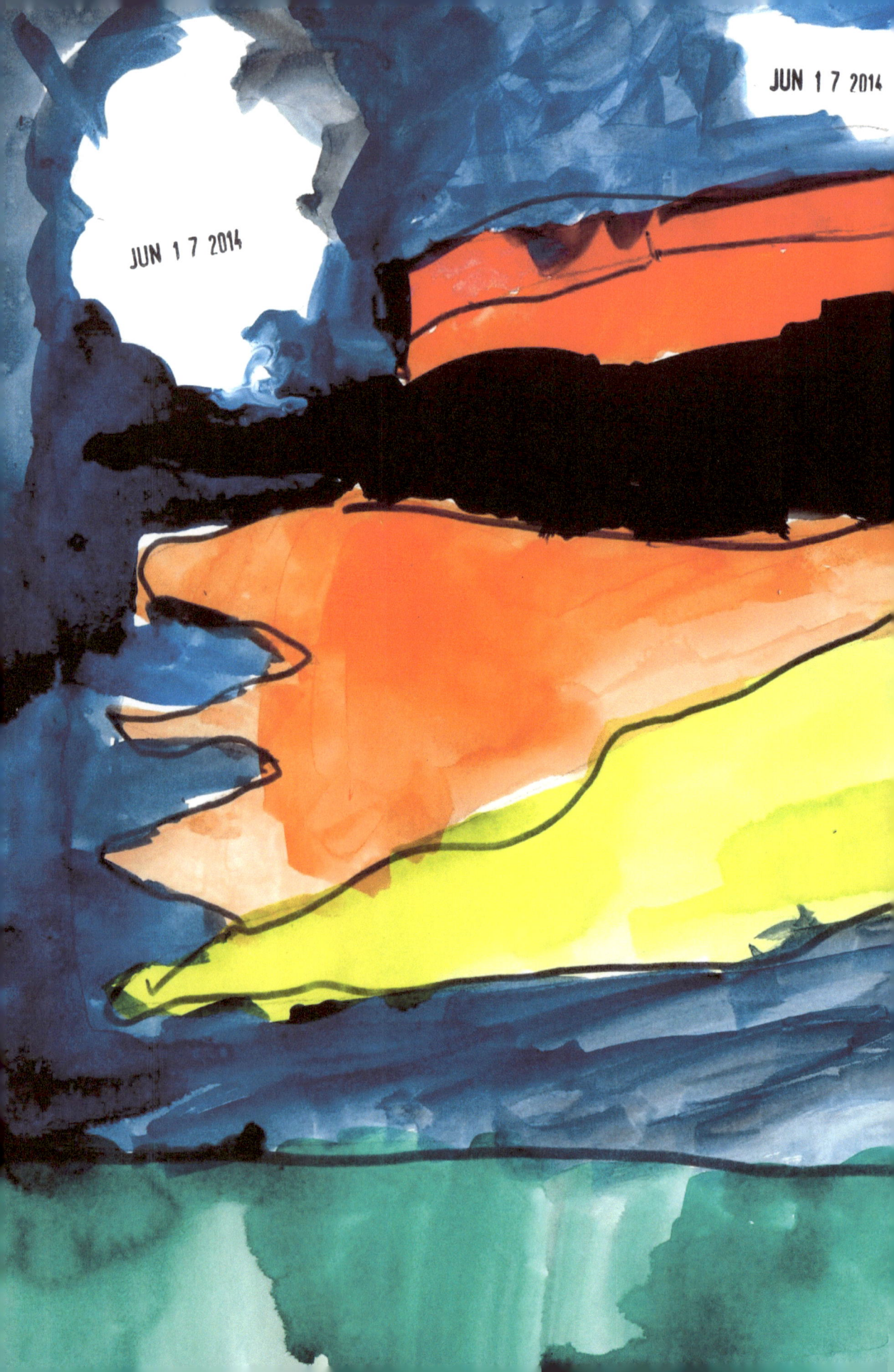

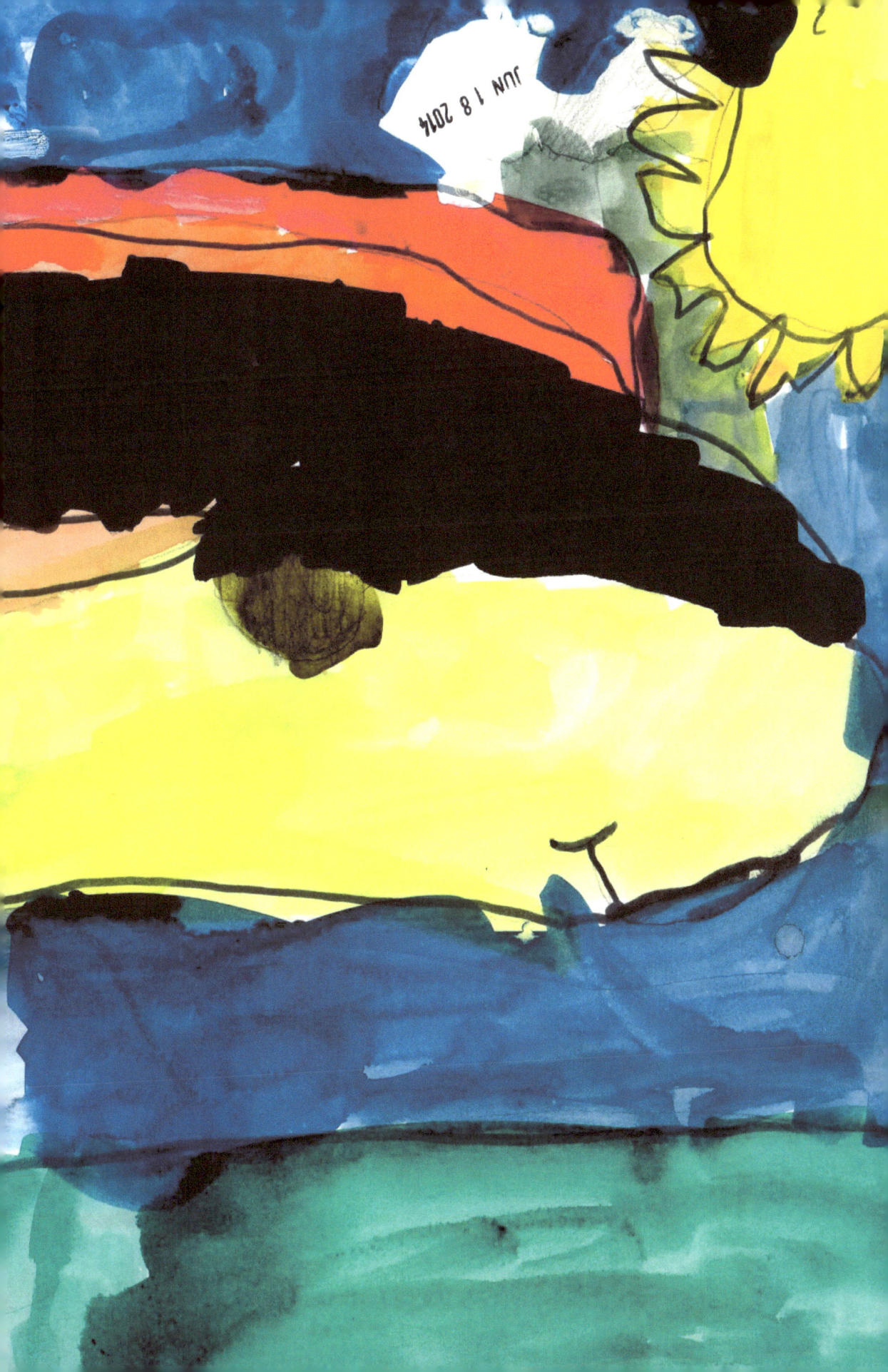
JUN 18 2014

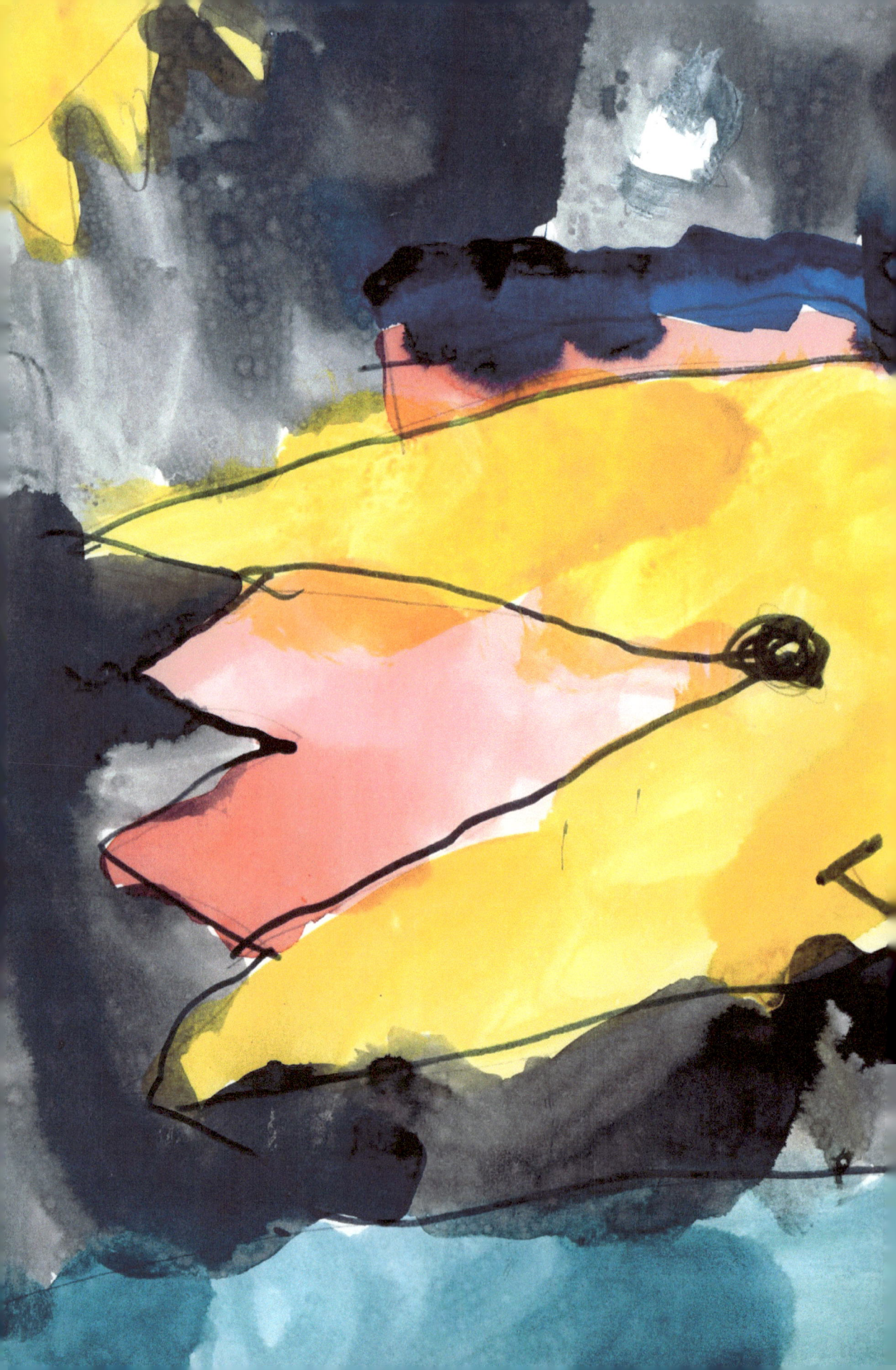

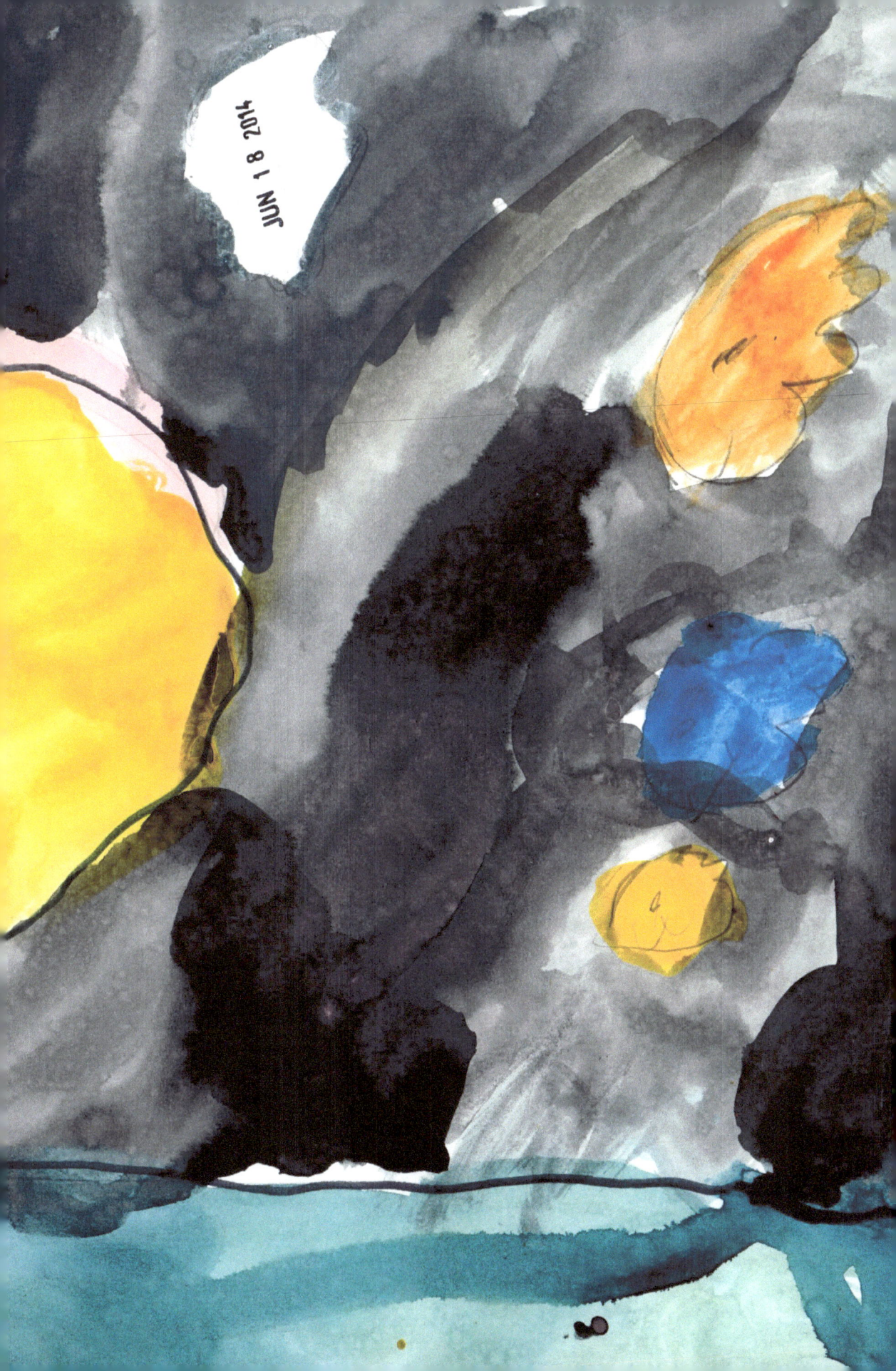

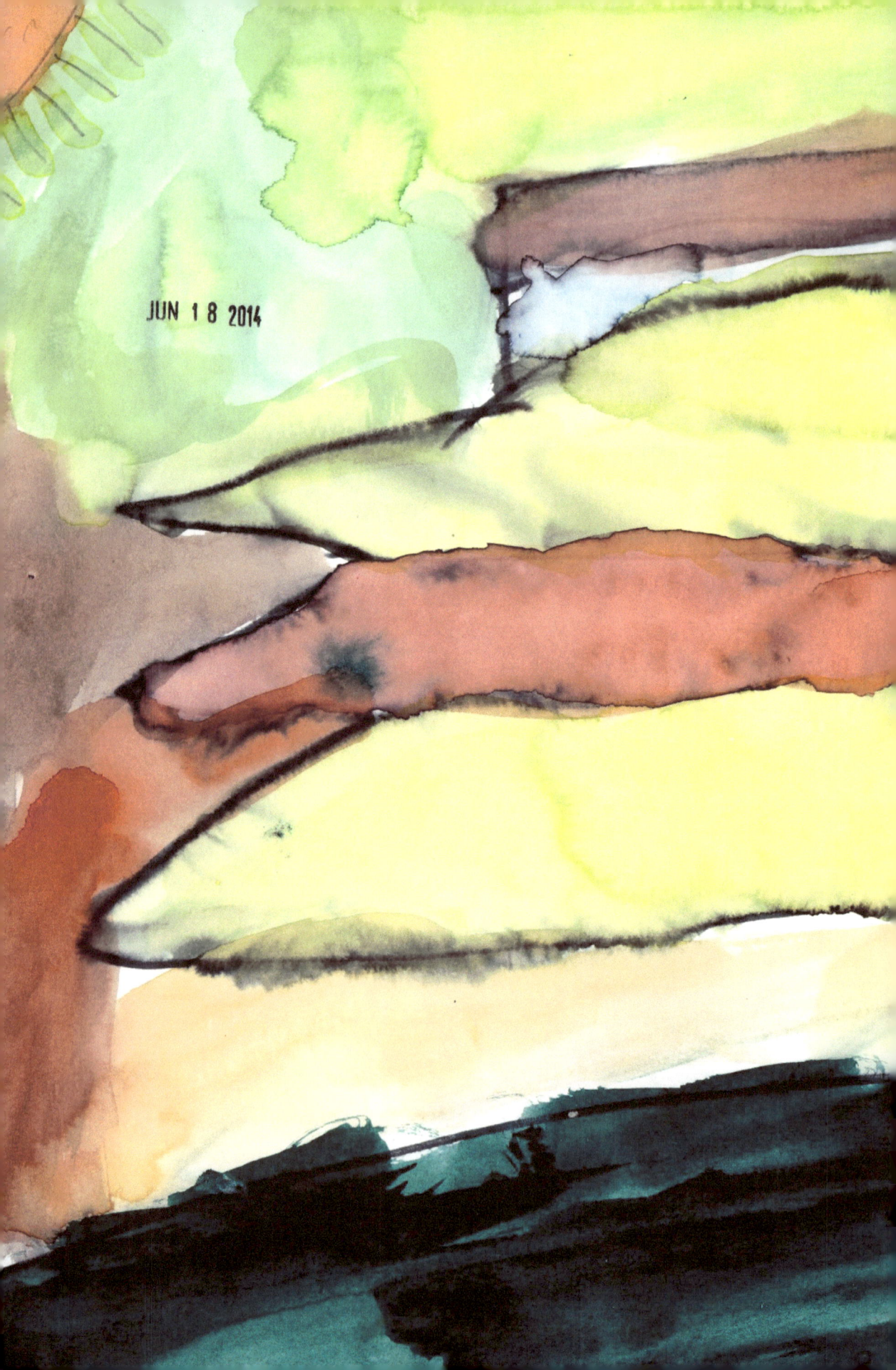

JUN 1 8 2014

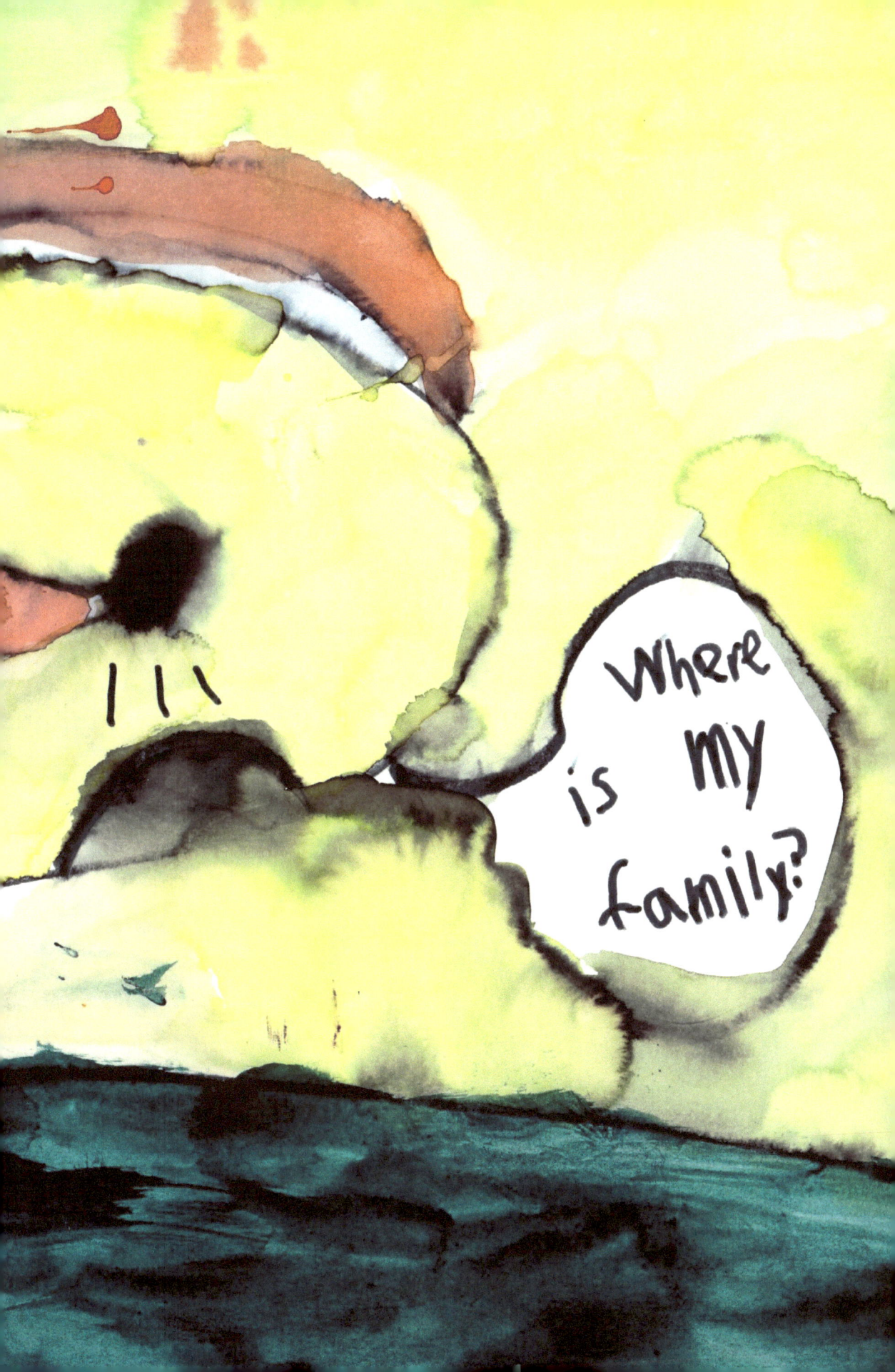

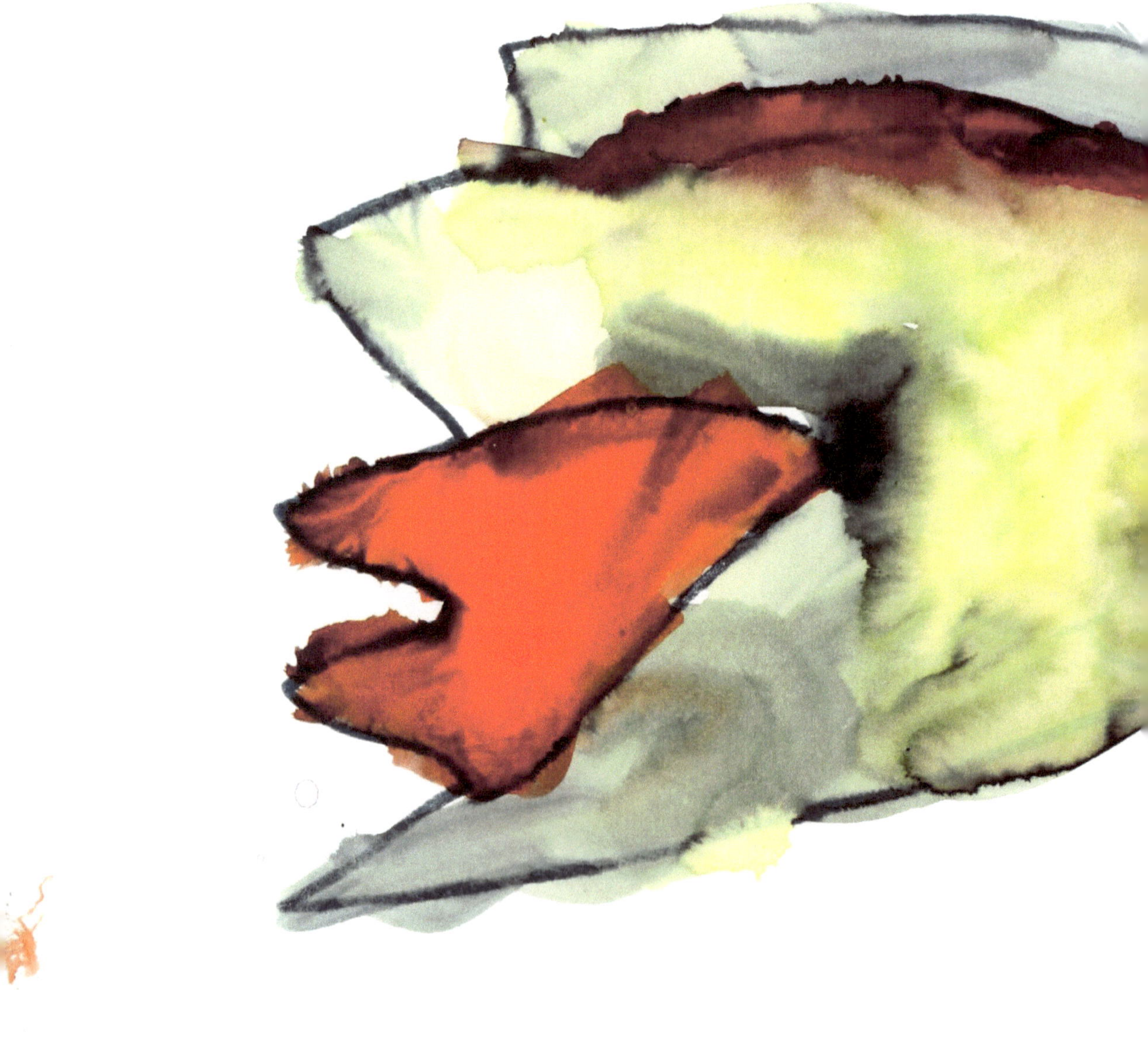

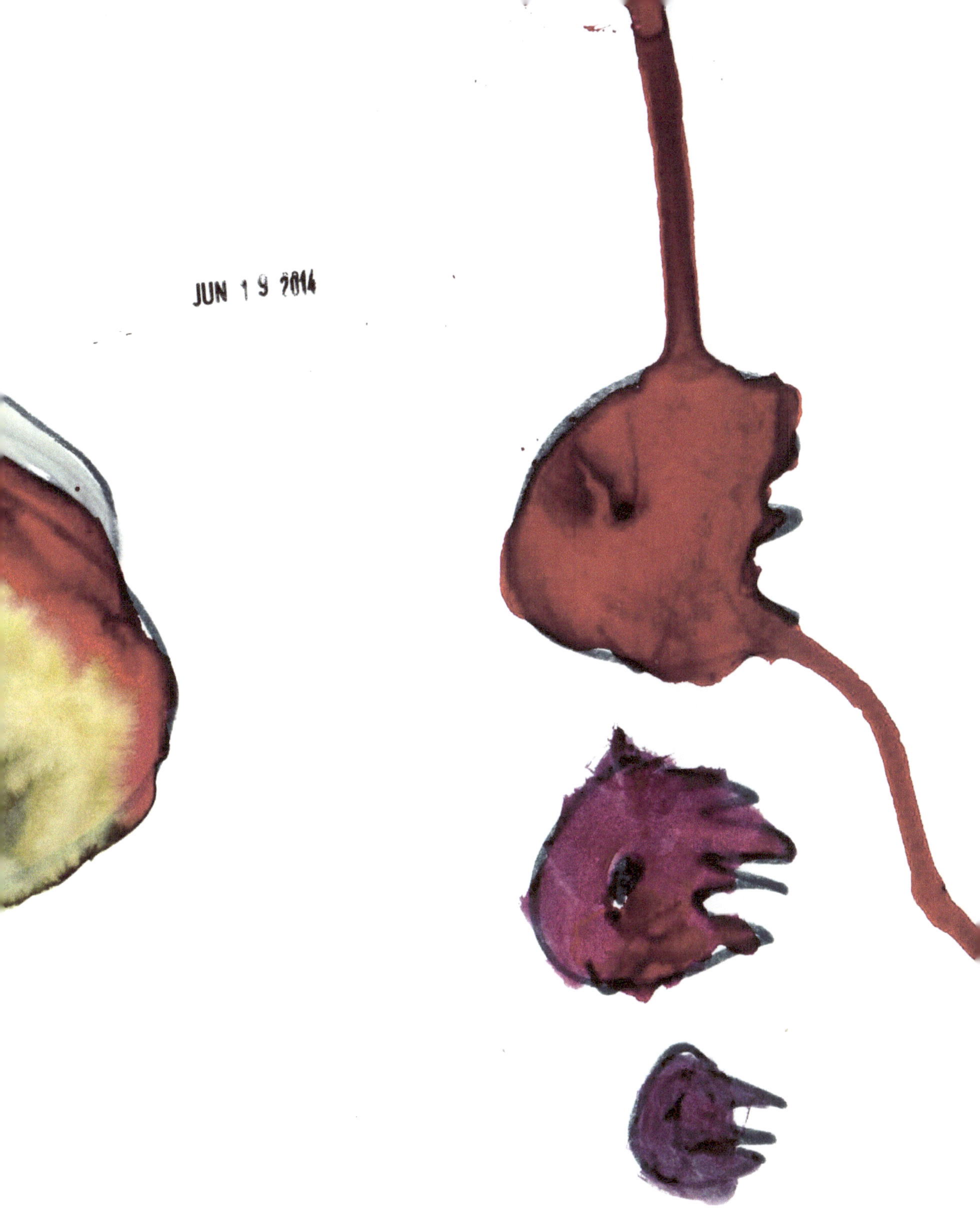

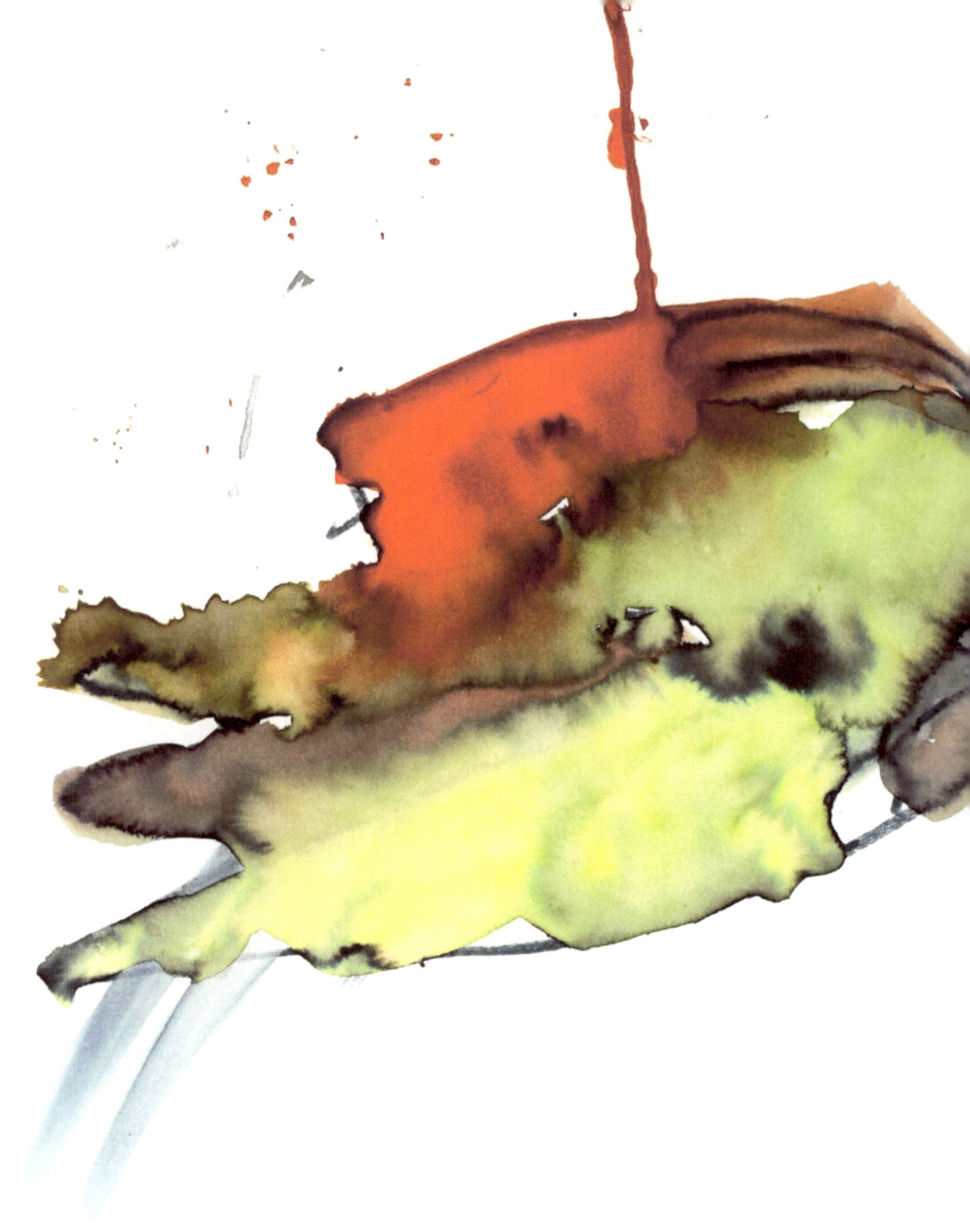

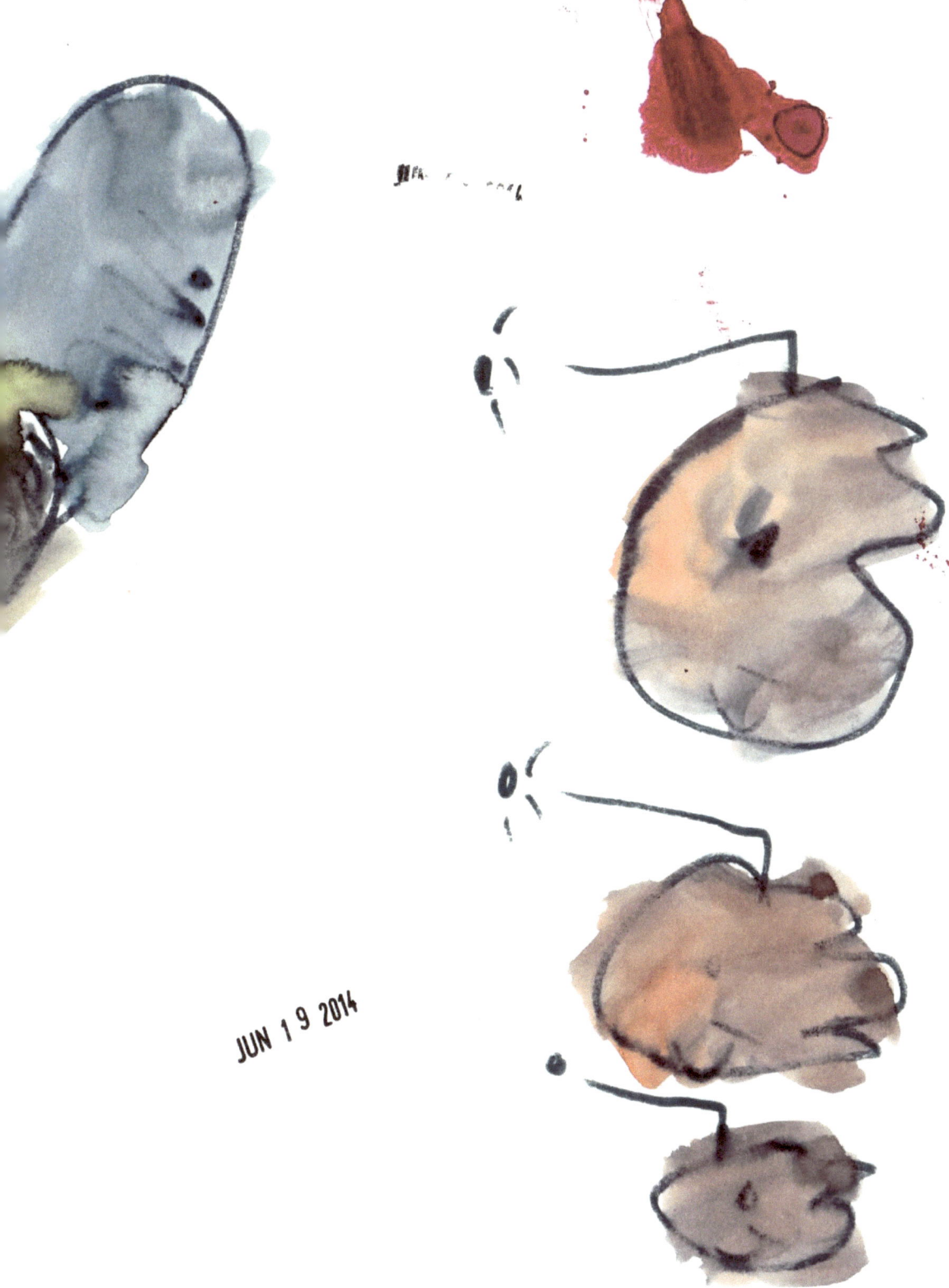

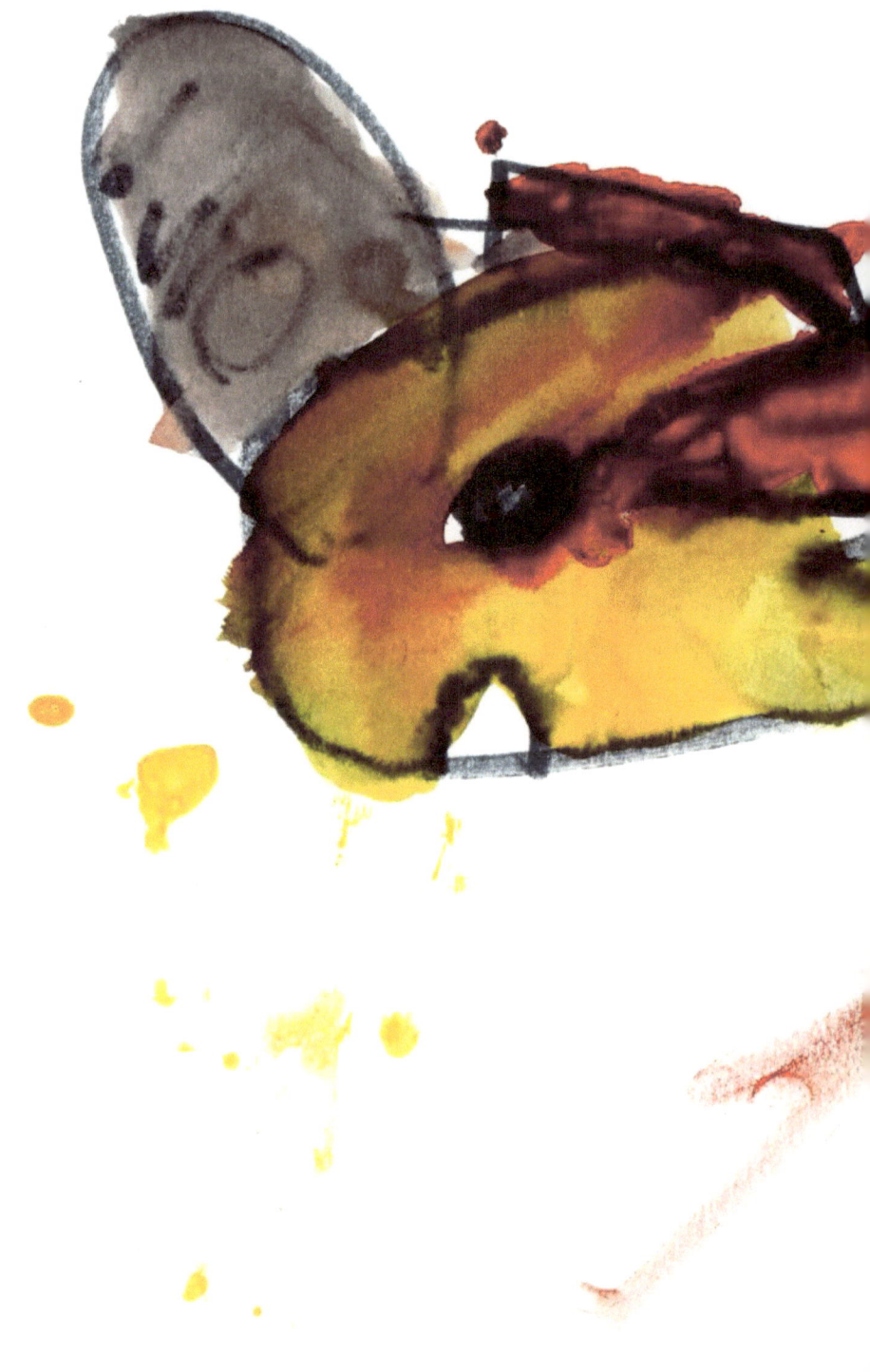

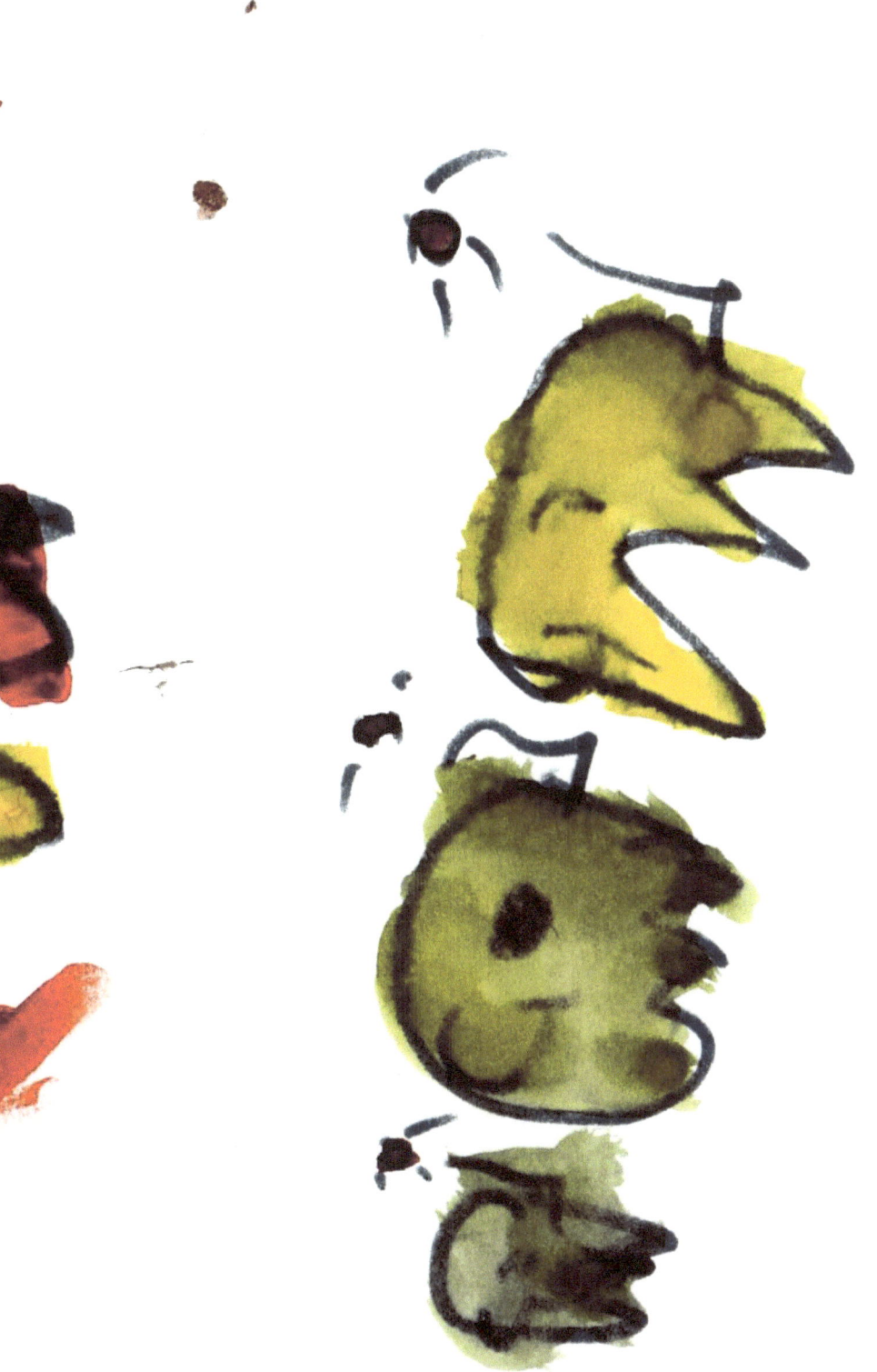

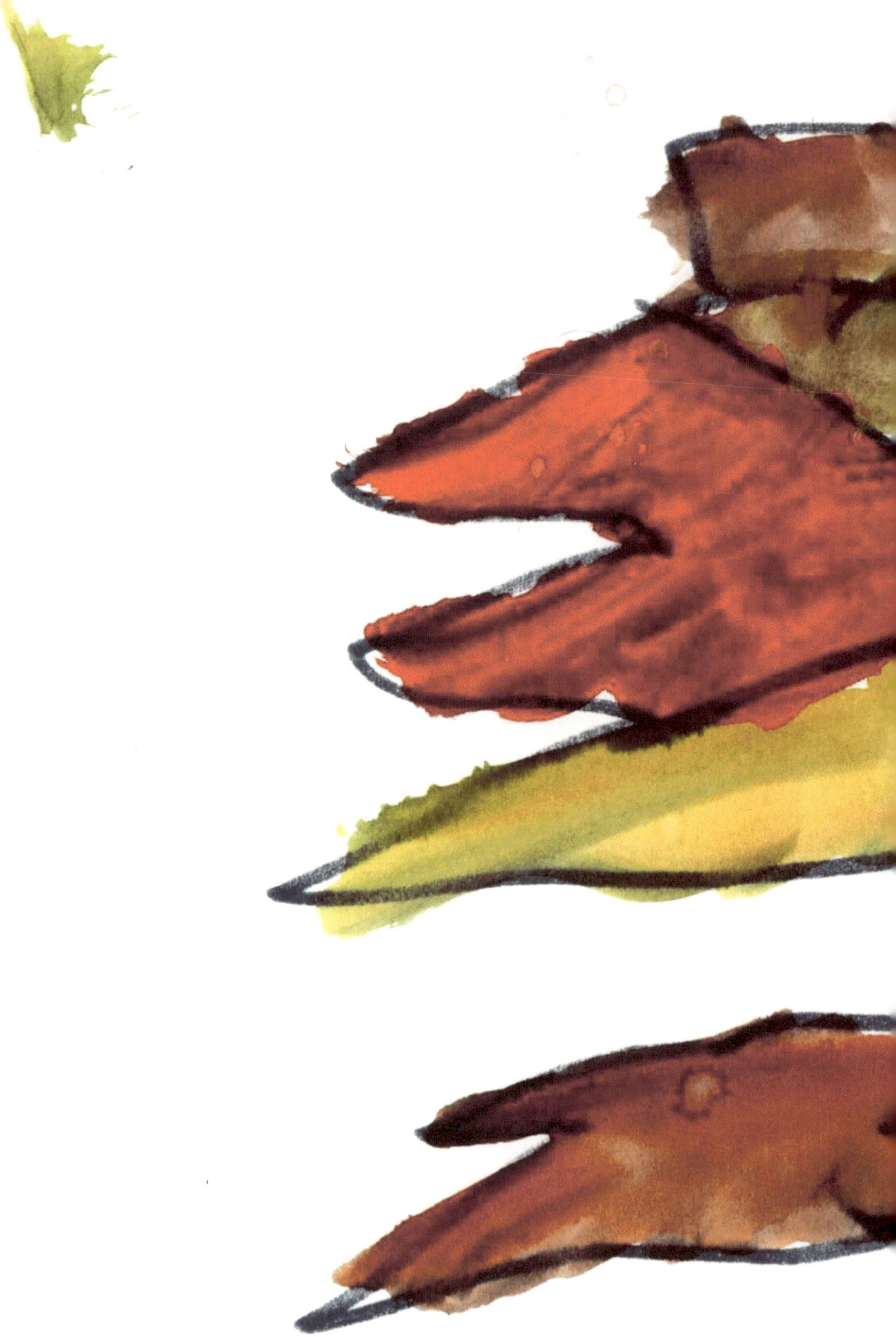

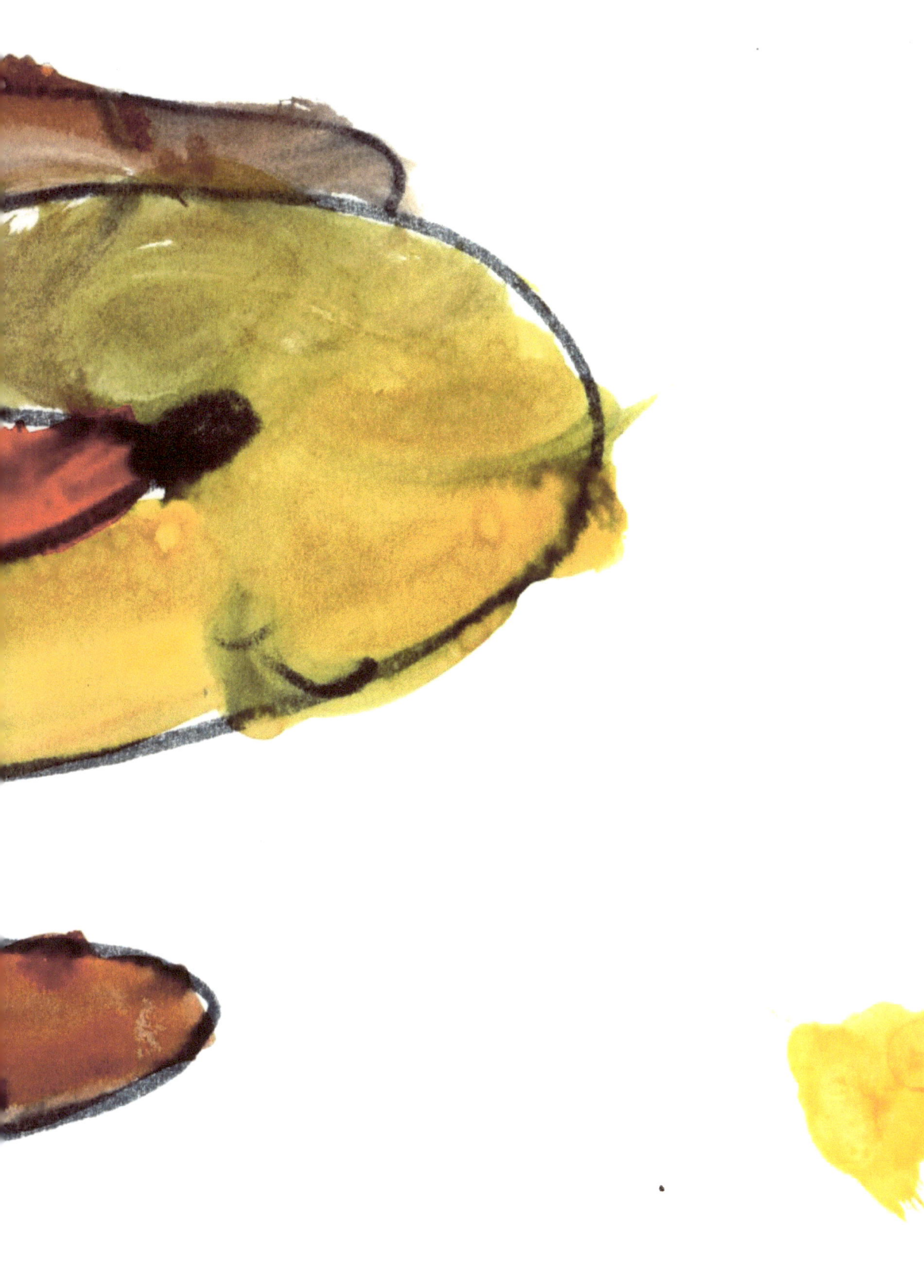

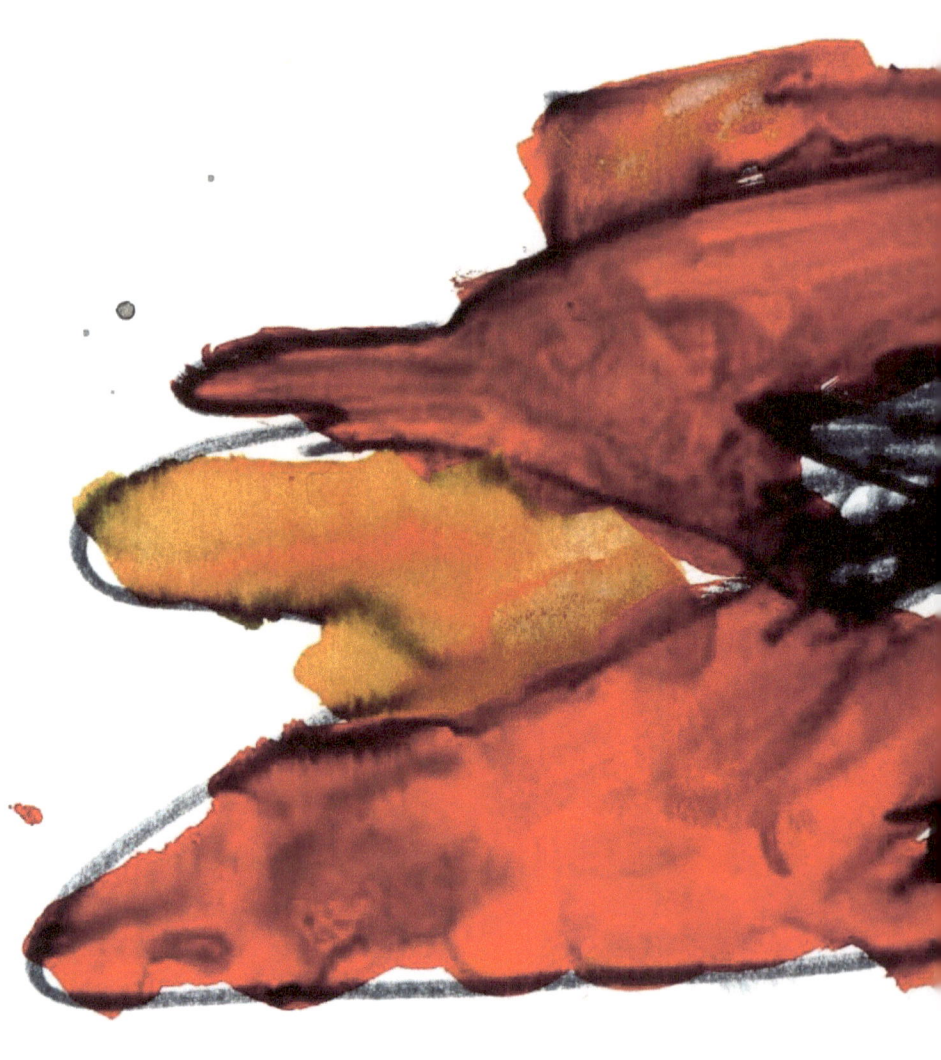

TO BE
CONTINUED

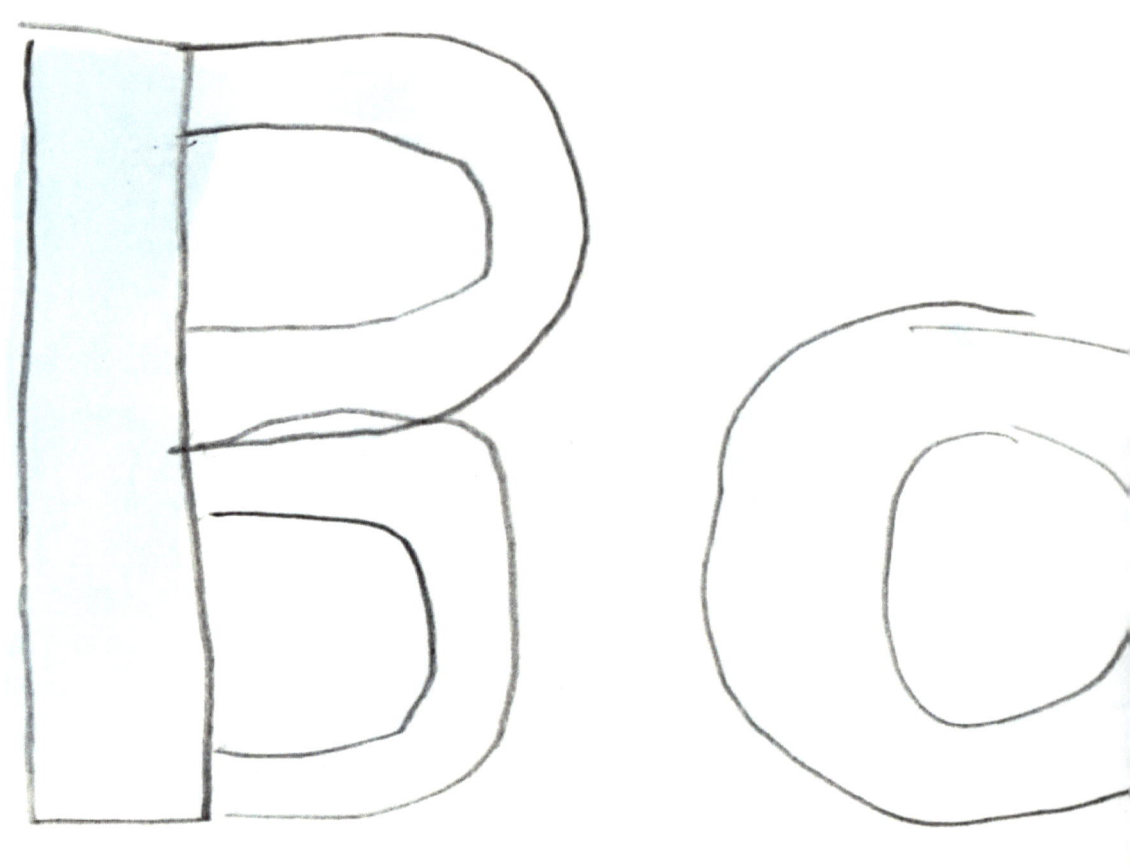

by Malachi

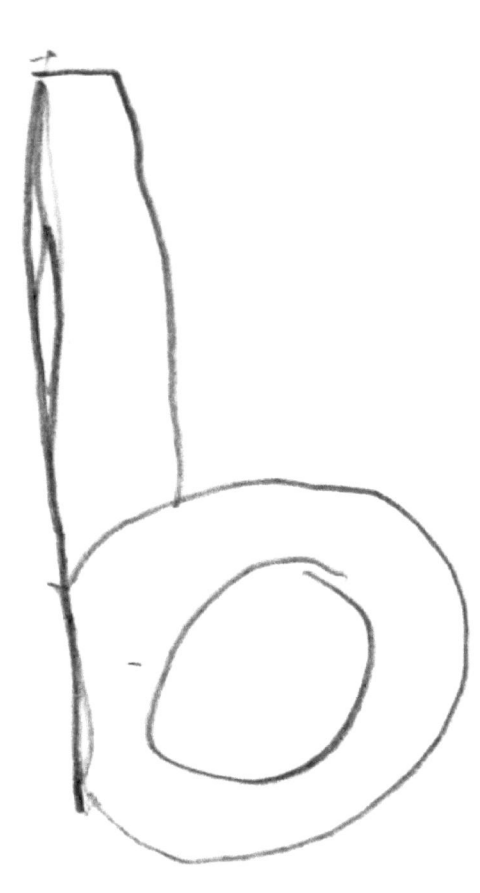

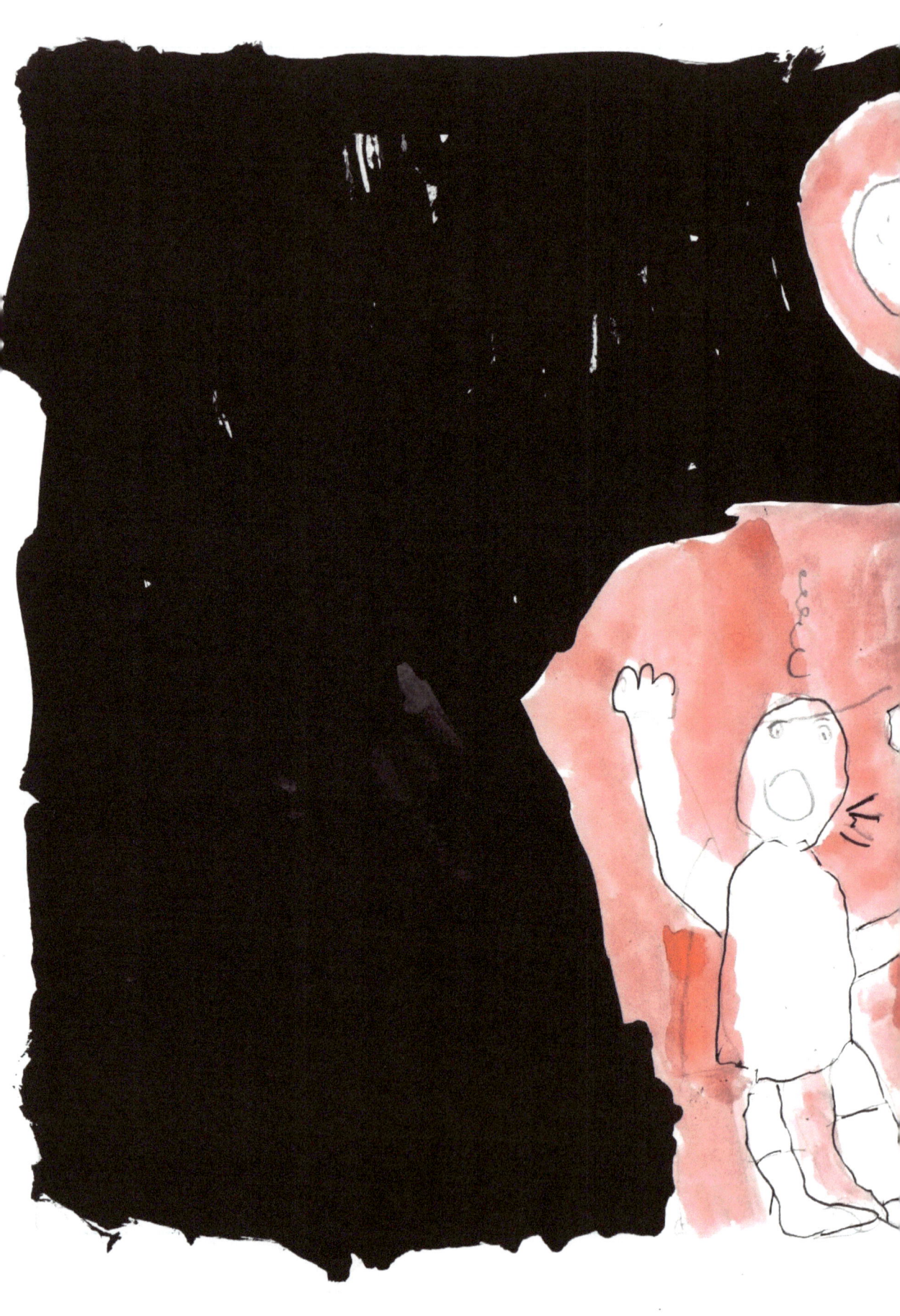

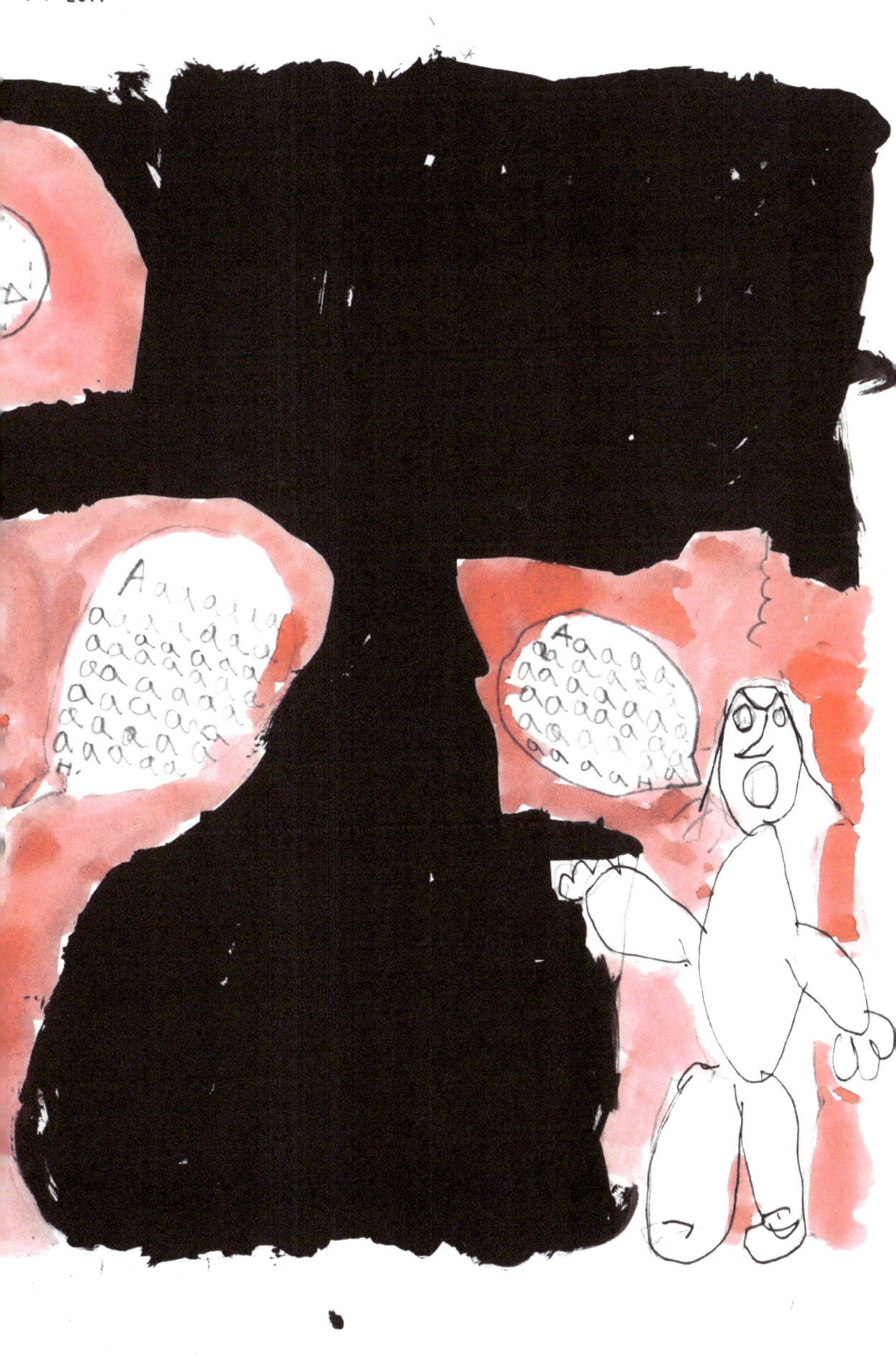

1 8 2014

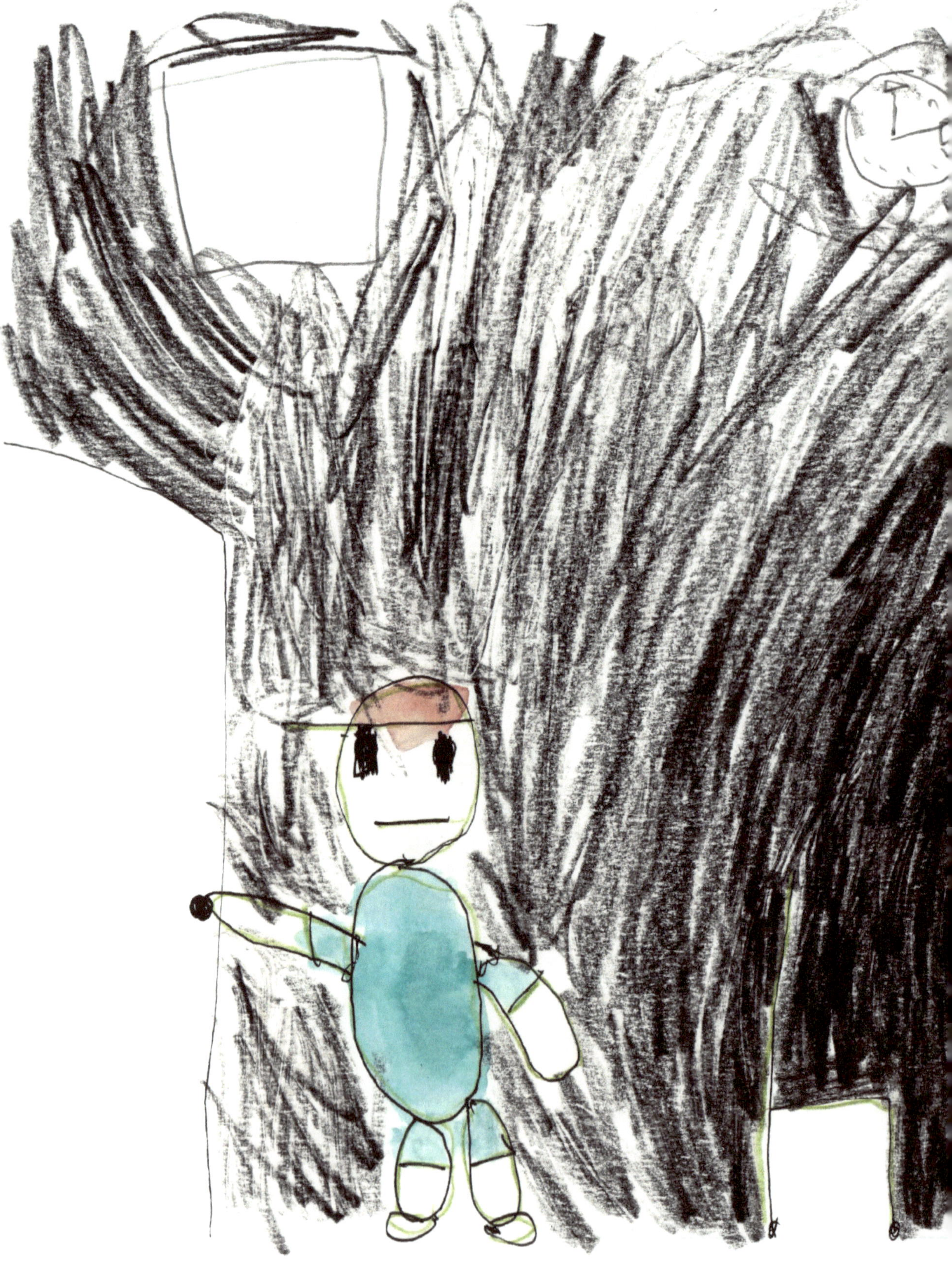

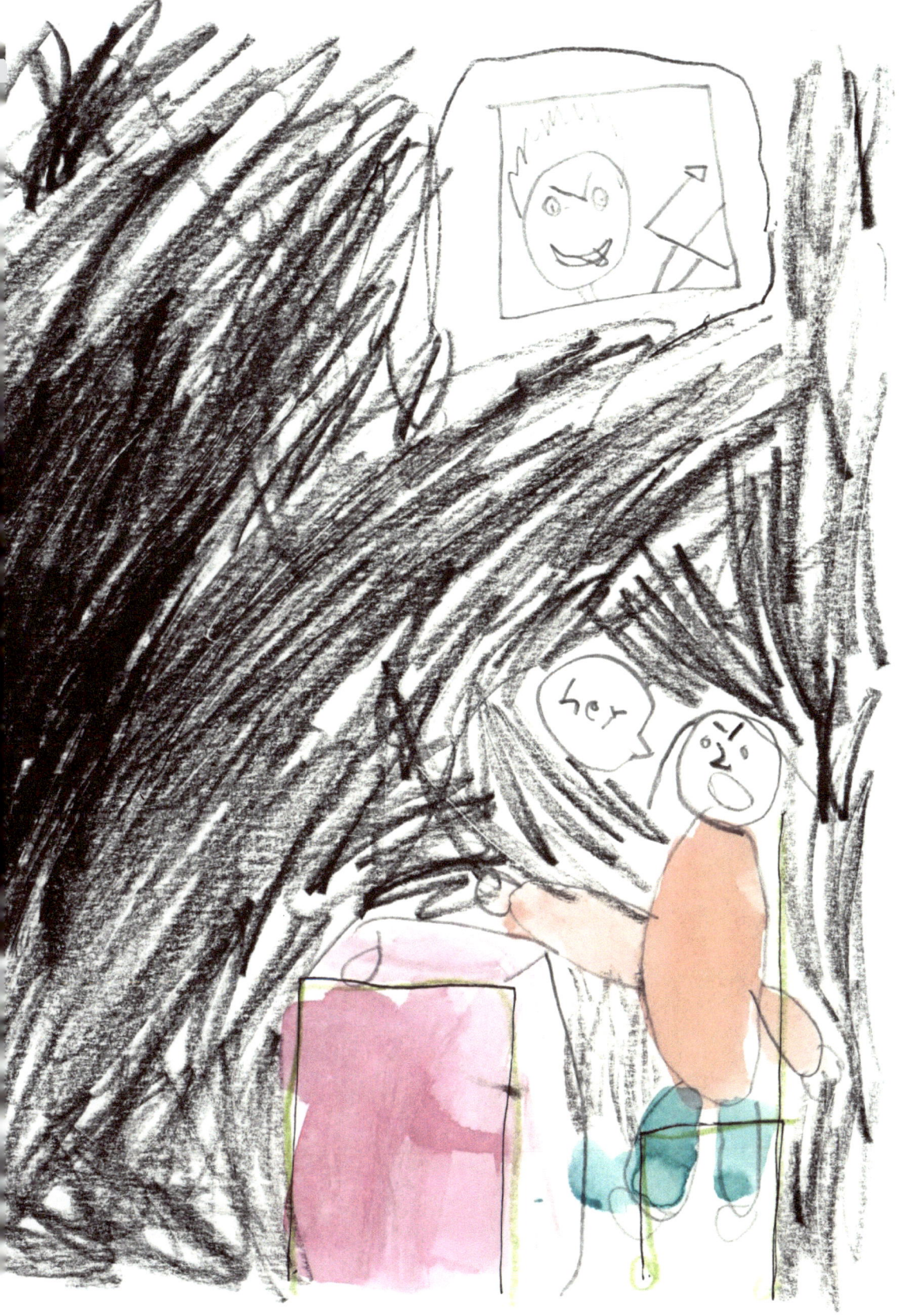

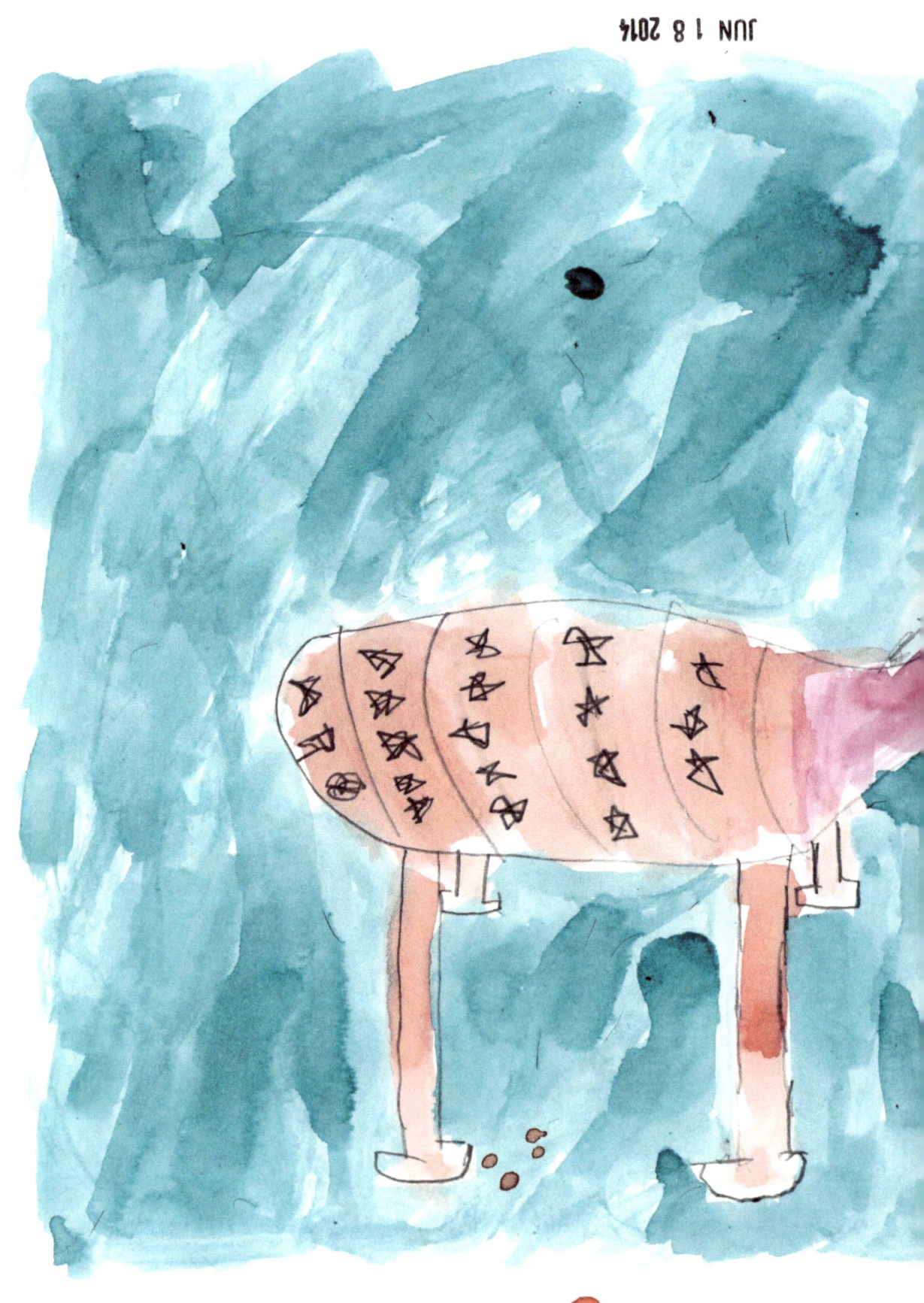

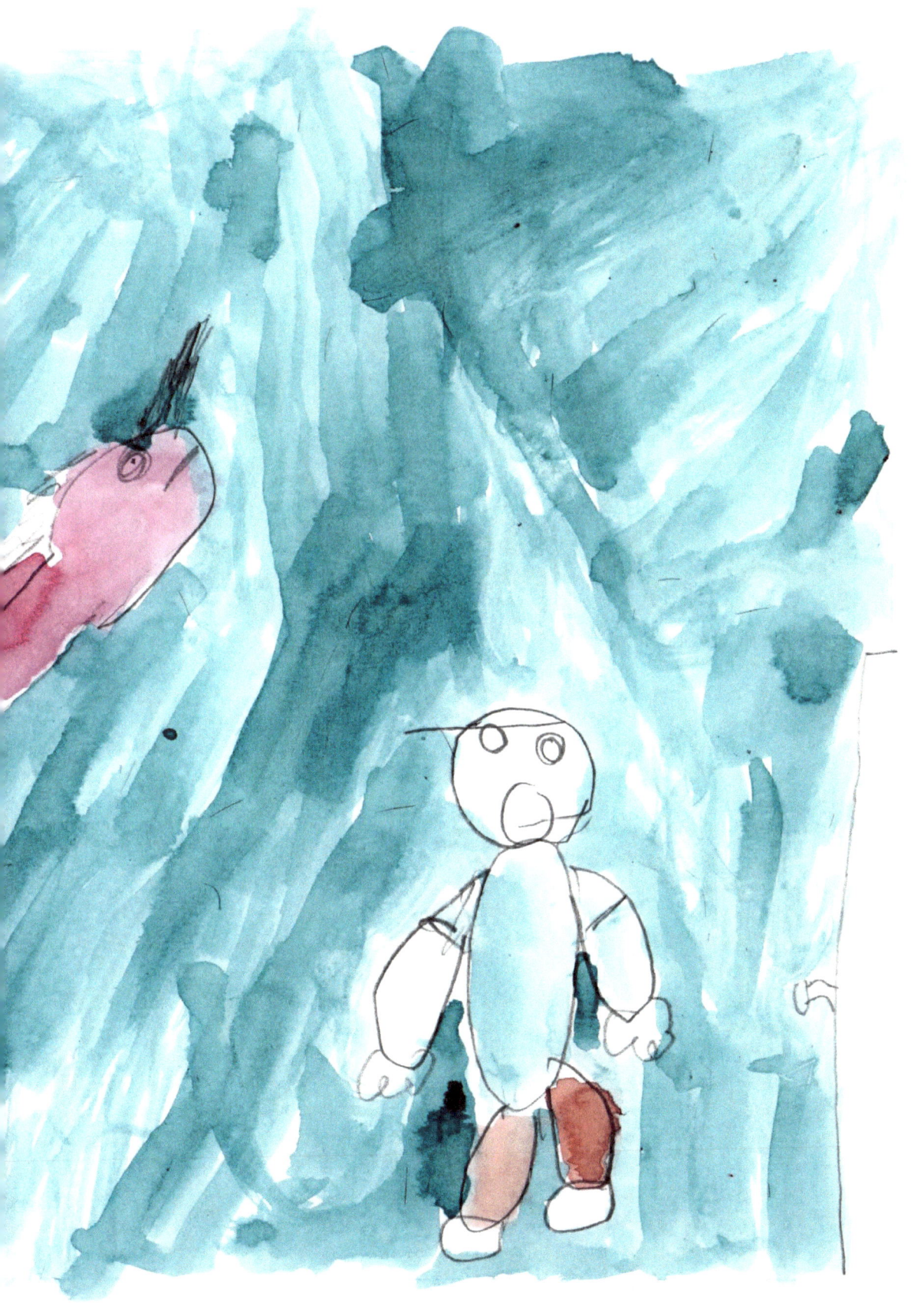

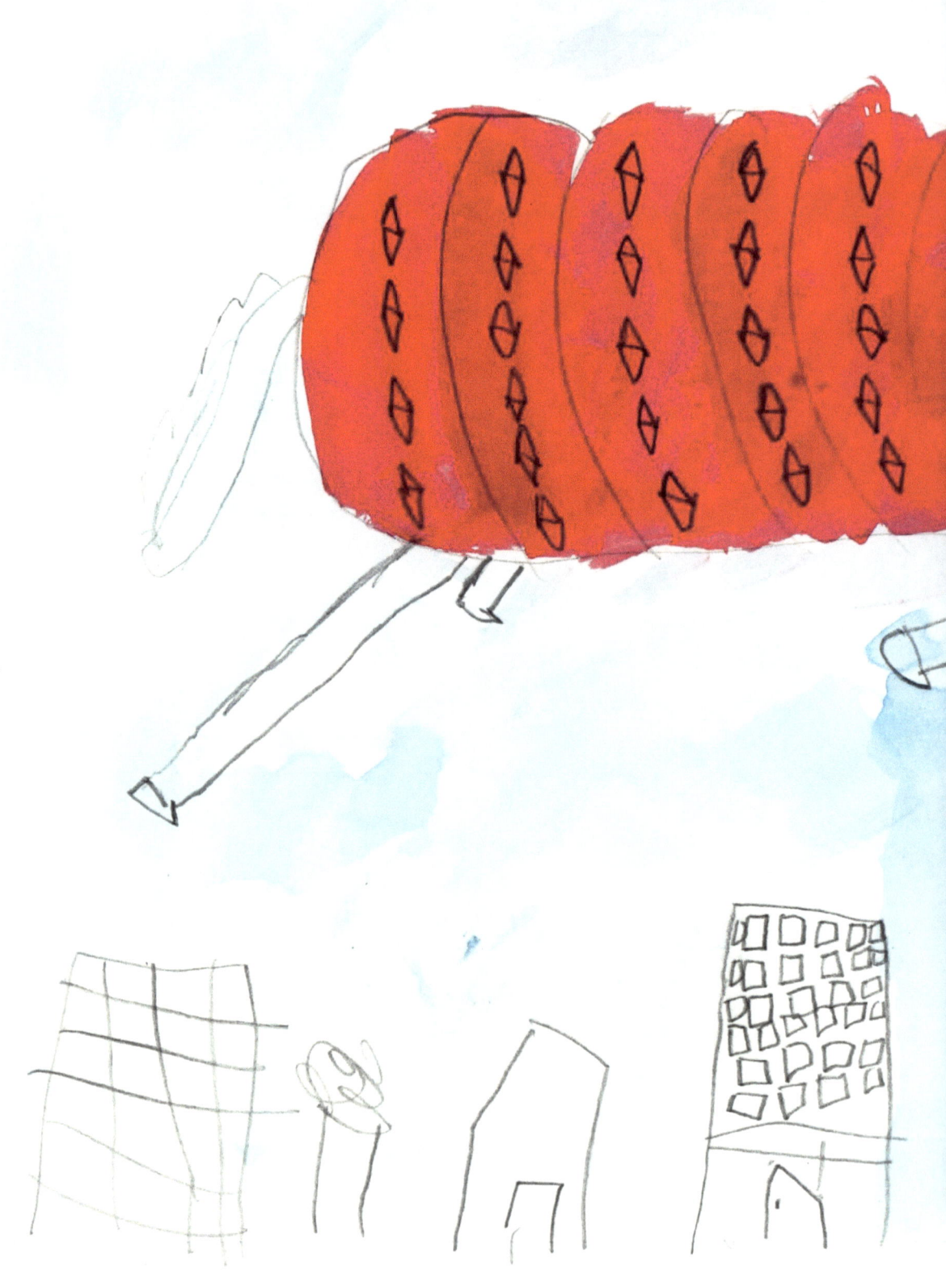

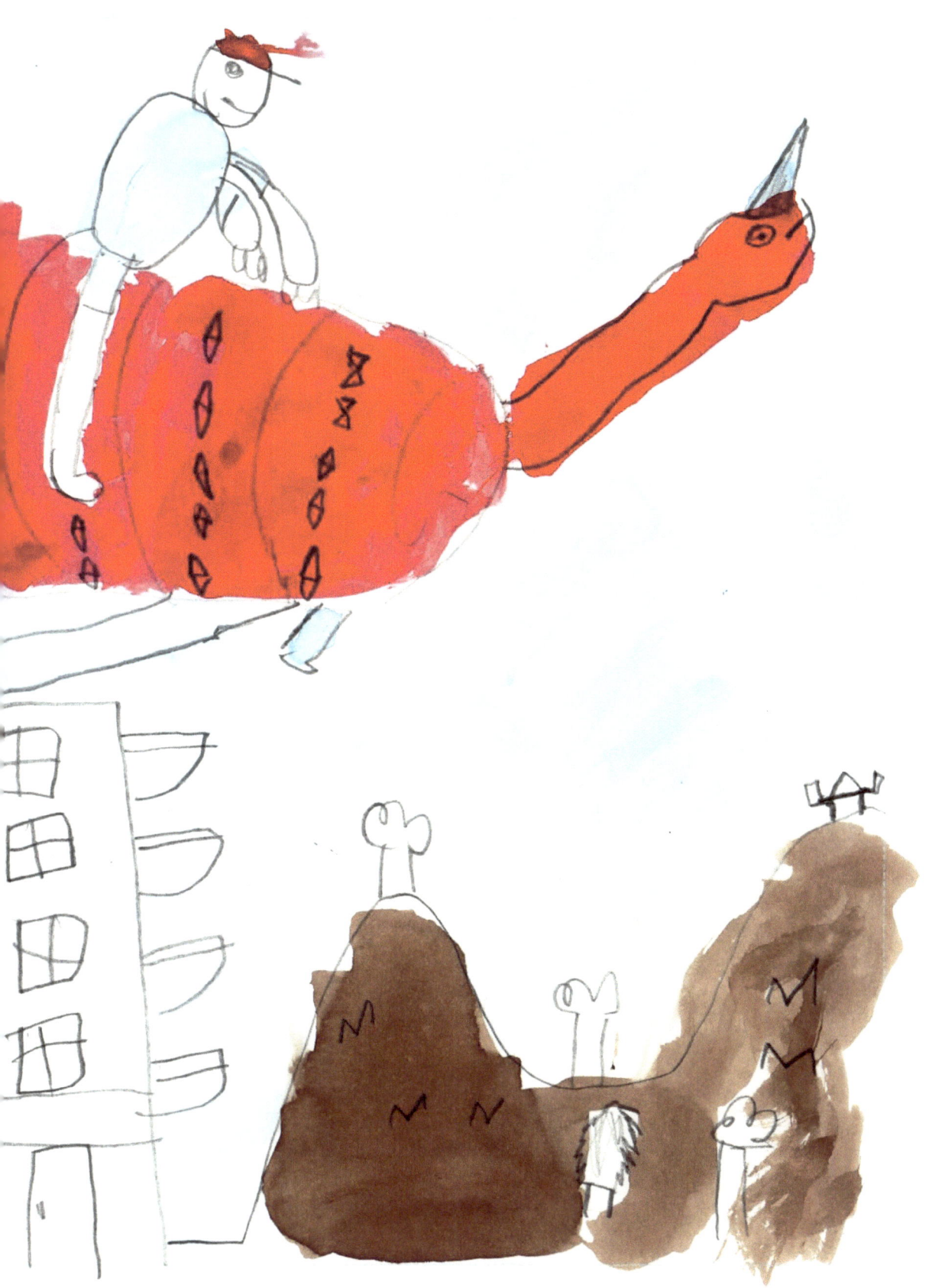

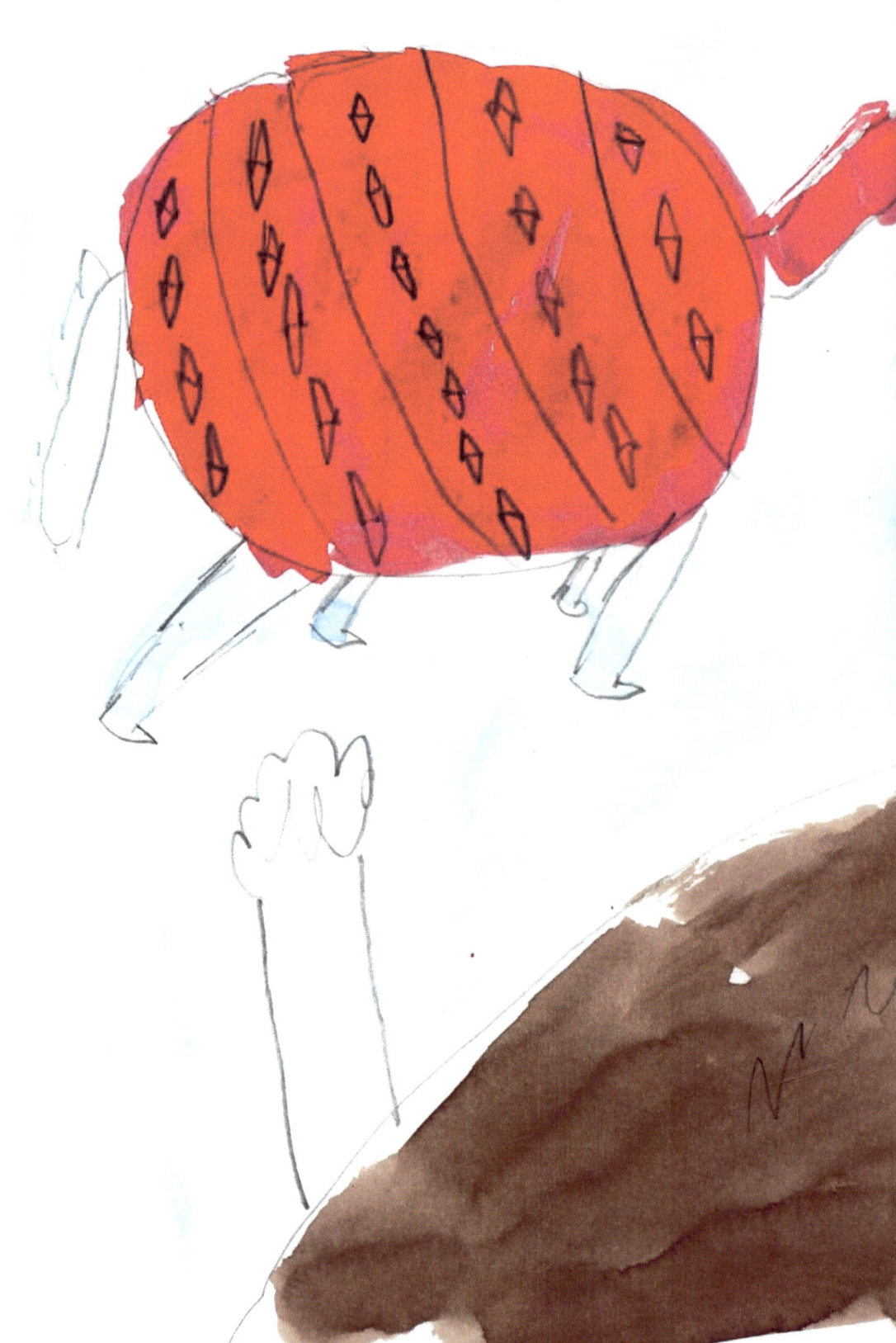

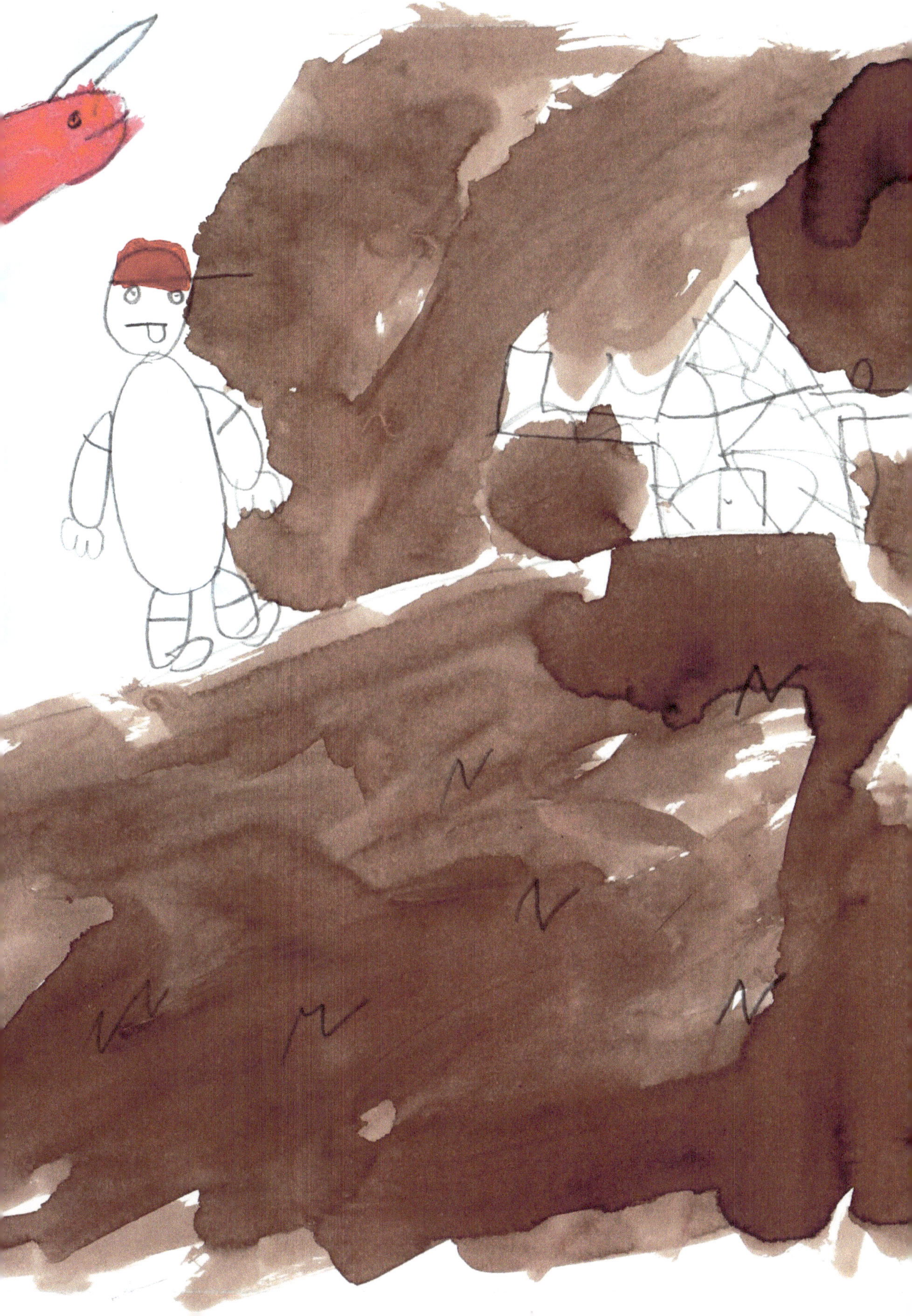

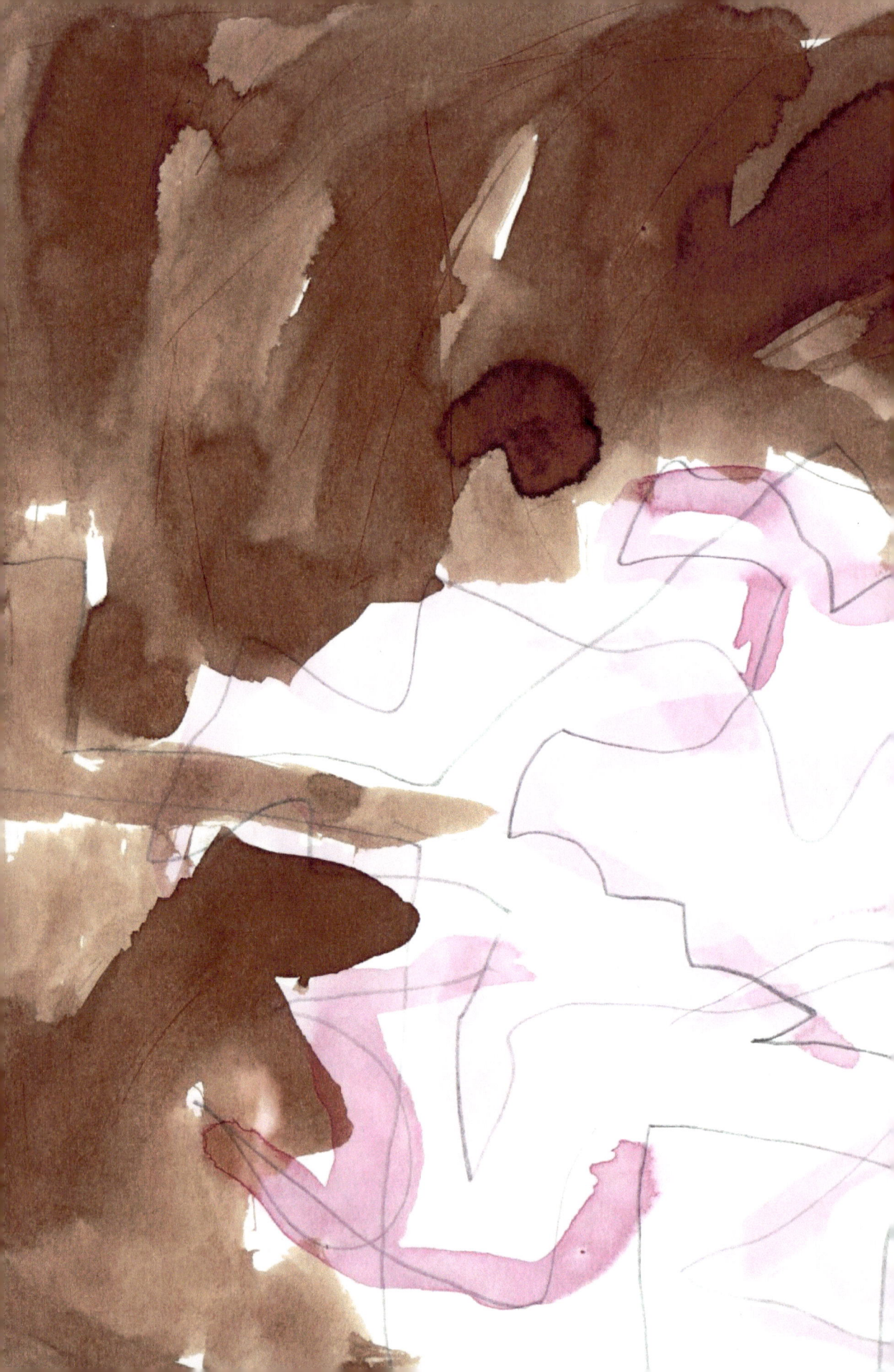

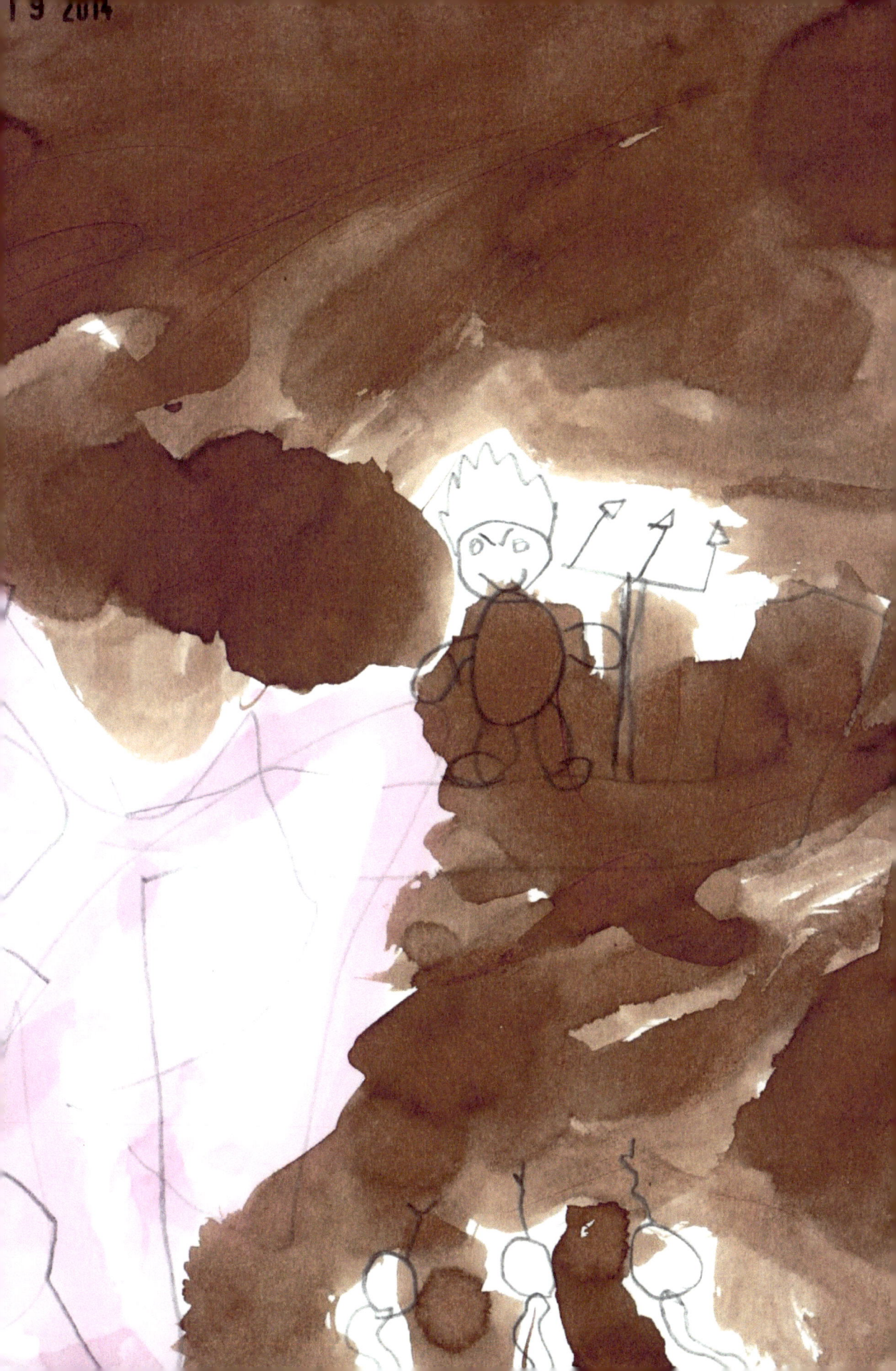

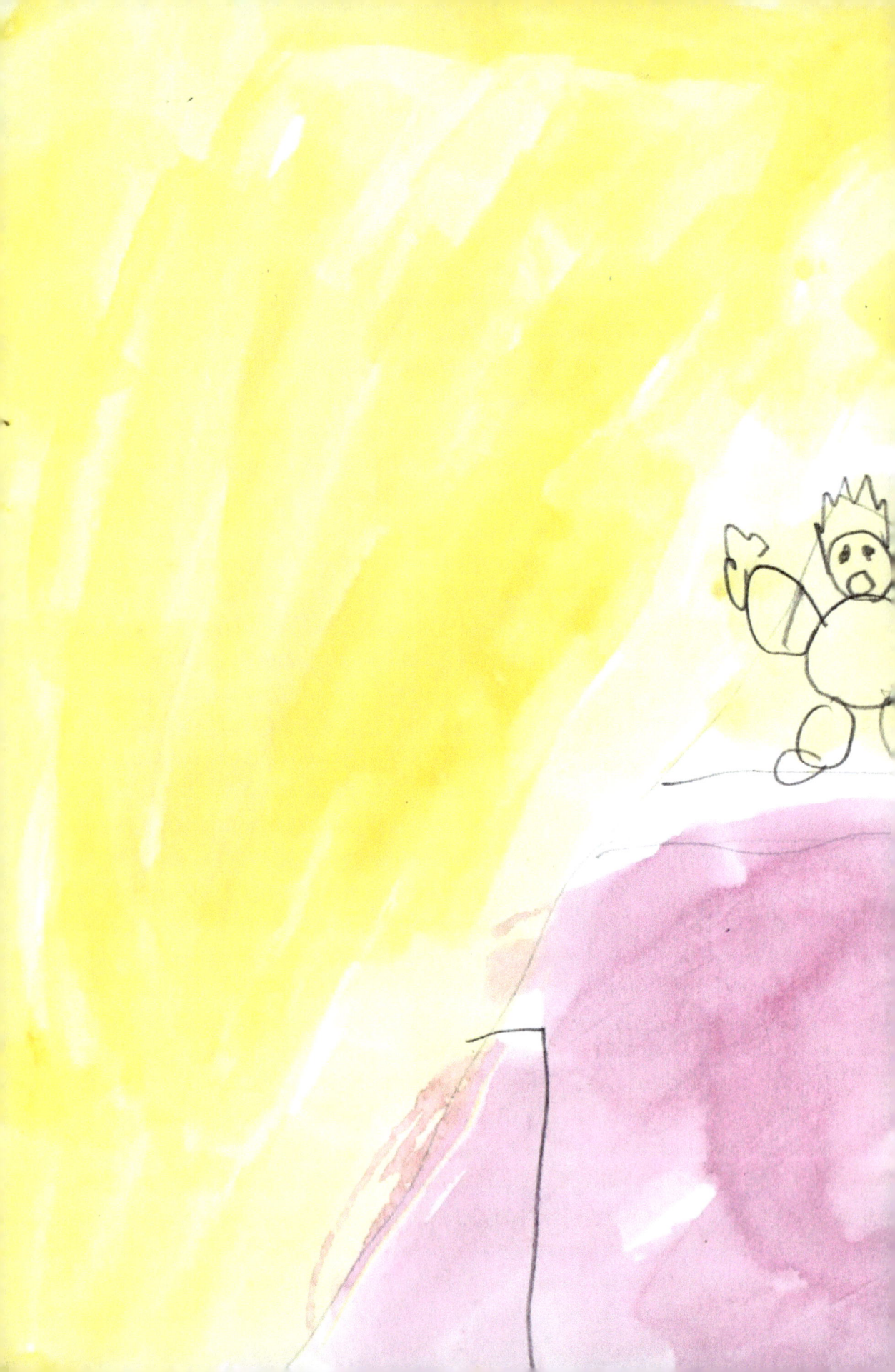

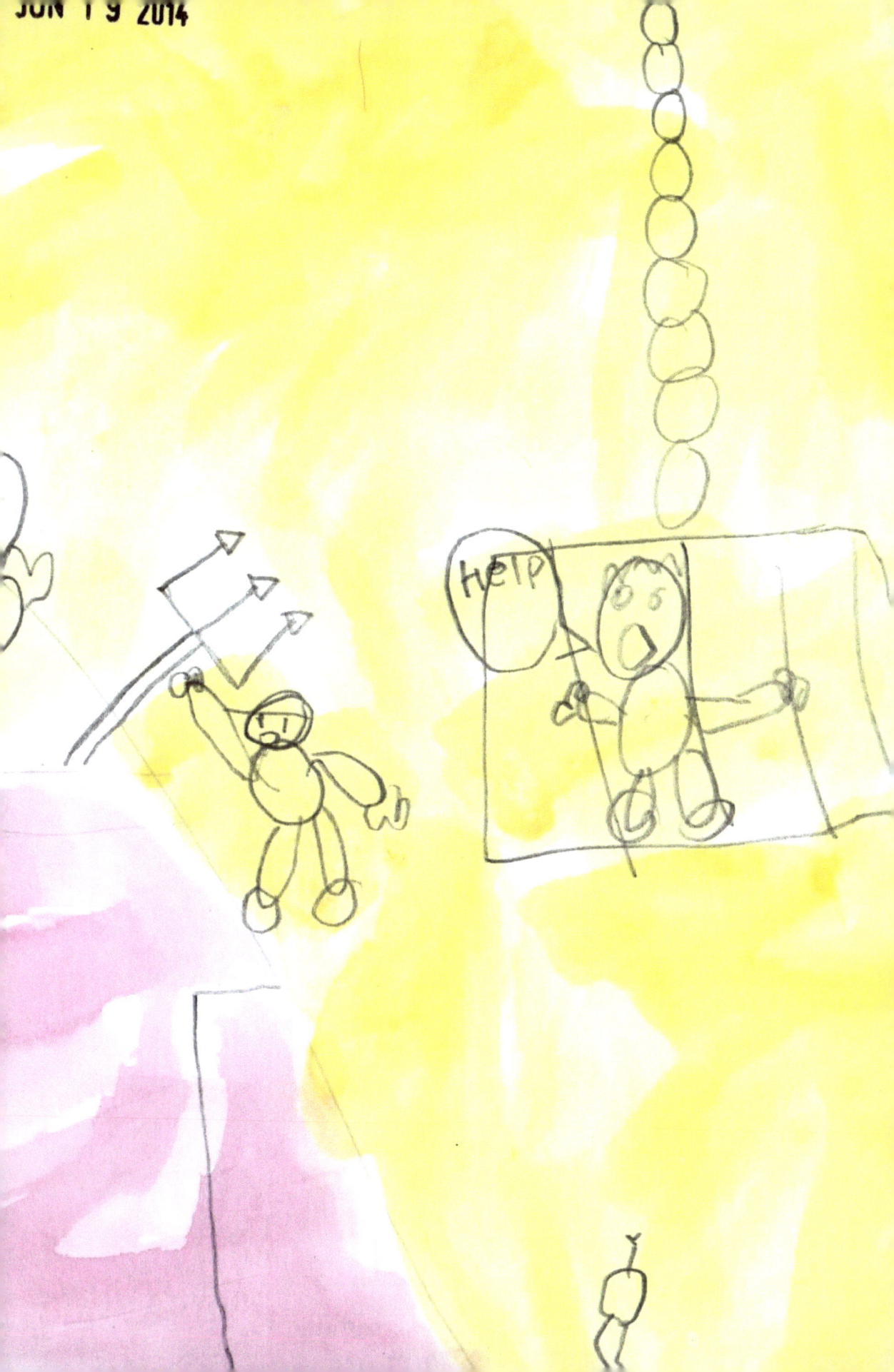

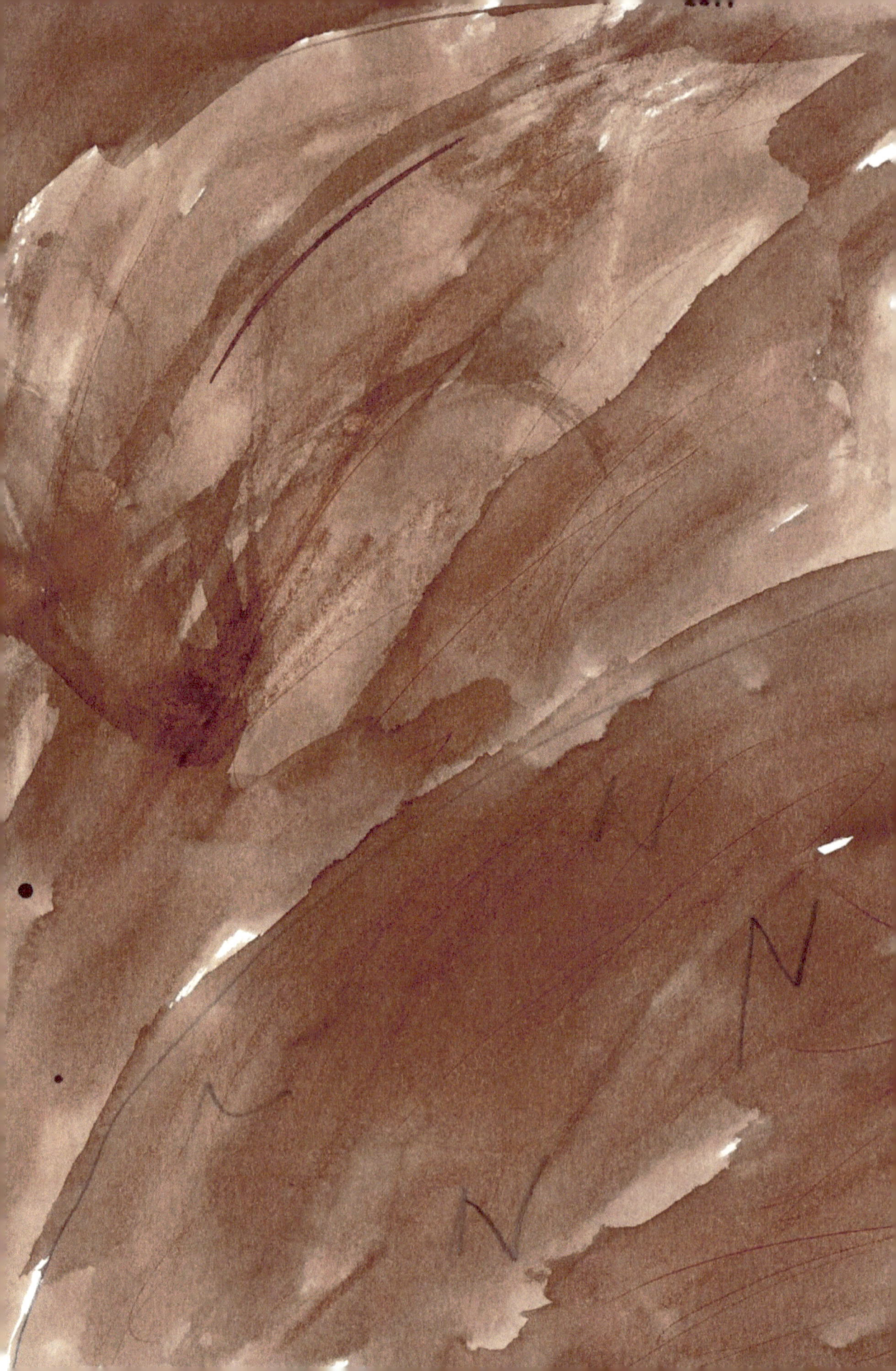

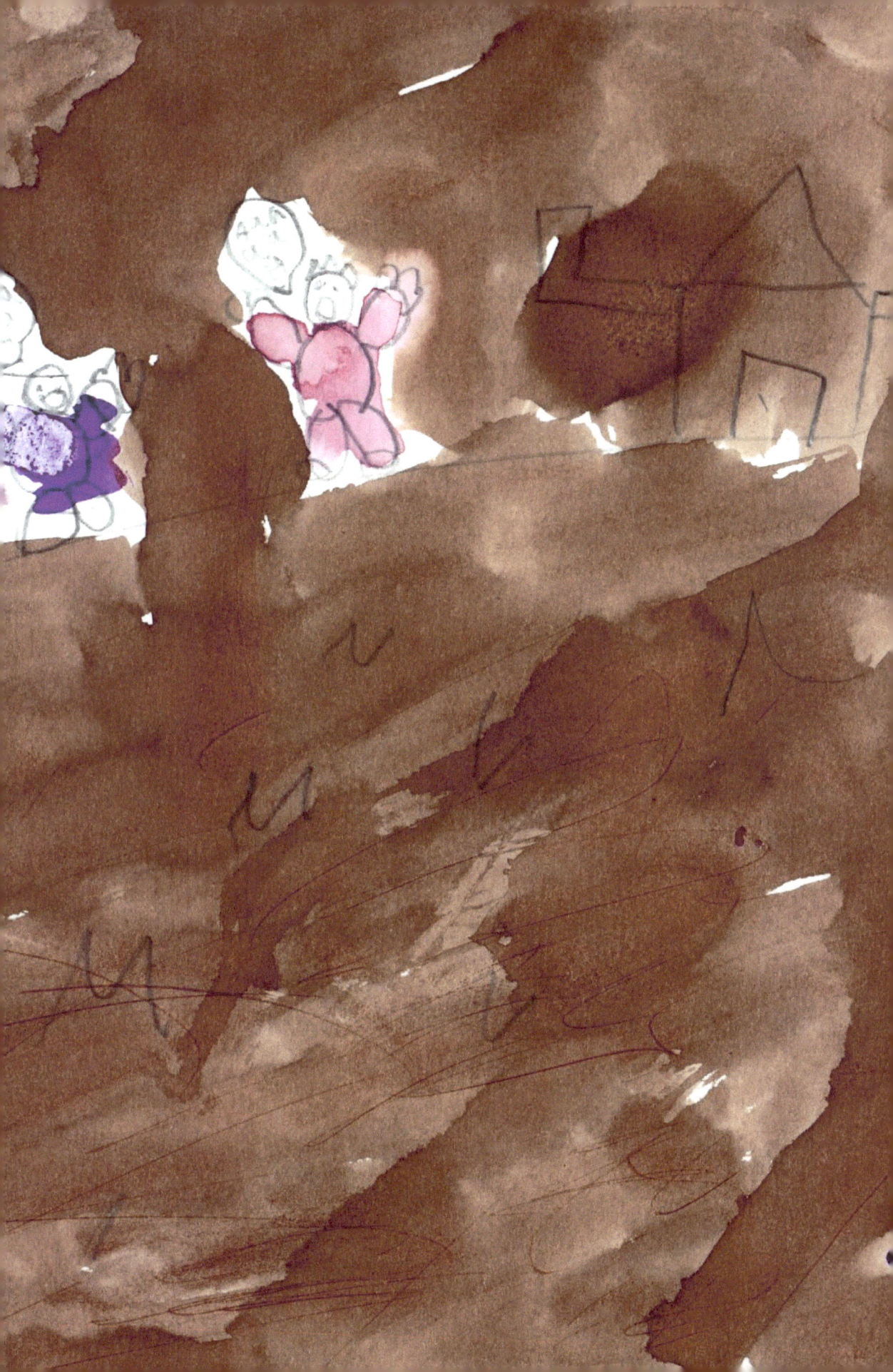

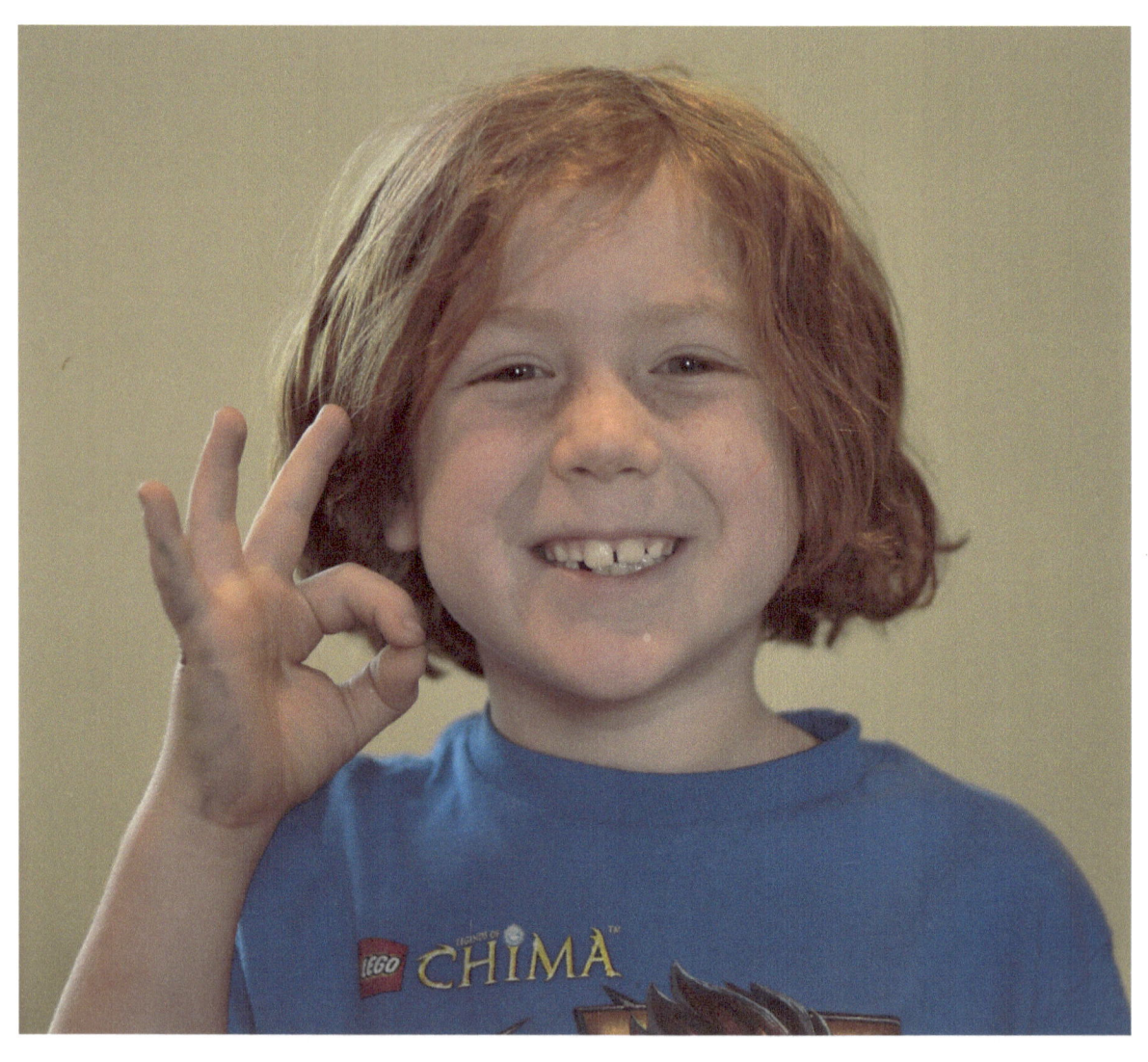

Torin Monaco

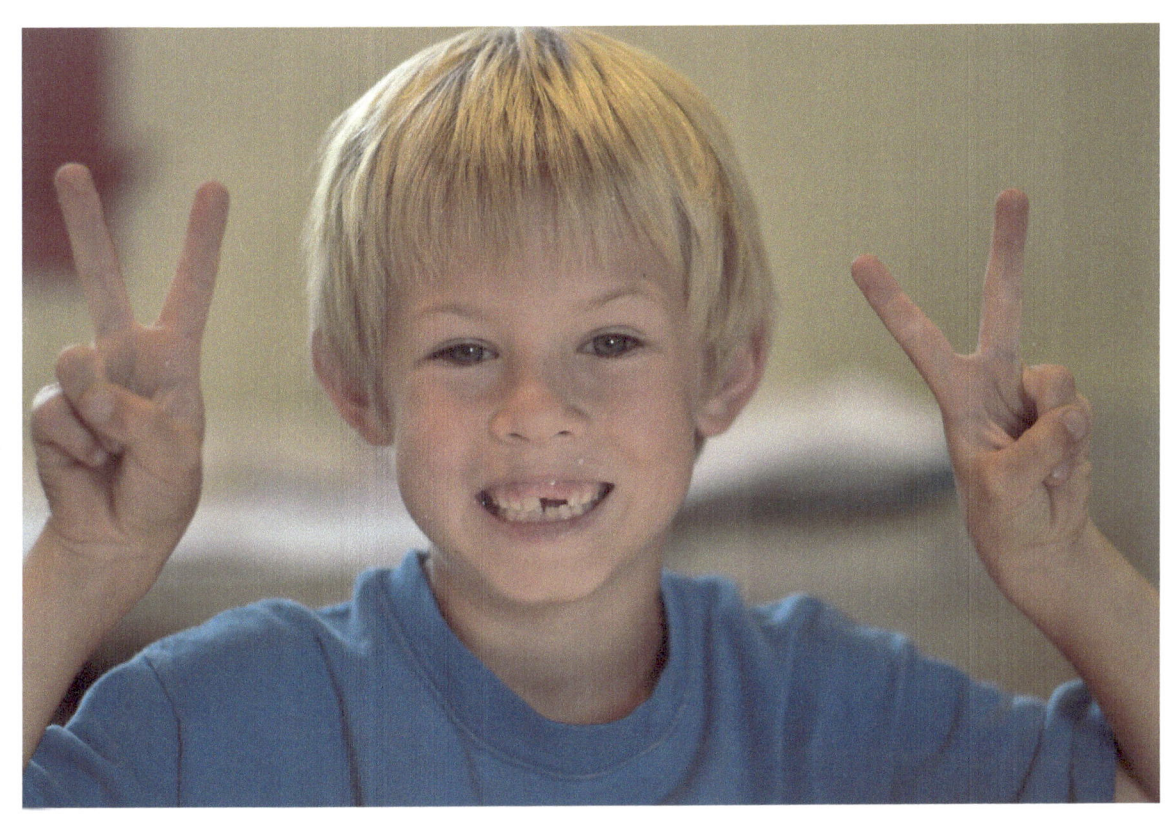

Malachi Keel